FIX THEM PLAIN OR FANCY,
BEANS ARE THE FLAVORFUL WAY
TO PUT HEALTH ON YOUR TABLE
. . . FOR PENNIES!

South-of-the-Border Black Bean Dip
For parties or snacks, this tangy dip goes great with fresh salsa and salt-free tortilla or veggie chips . . . and you can mix it up in just three minutes.

Kidney Bean, Chicken, and Mango Salad
A delicious eight-minute marvel, this perfect summer meal looks beautiful on a bed of shredded romaine lettuce and tastes superb . . . a magnificent mix of flavors!

Split Pea and Spinach Soup
Sure to become a favorite for winter lunches, this satisfying "second-helping-good" soup is a nutrient-rich crowd pleaser.

Mexican Lasagne
A low-cost meal that can serve six, this unconventional, meatless version of lasagne will bring you bravos . . . and no one will guess that it's exceptionally high in fiber and nearly fat-free.

Lentil and Orange Salad
The brilliant contrast of the slightly nutty lentils with the sweet-and-sour orange makes this fast-to-fix lunch or first course an exotic treat.

Light-style Baked Beans with Ham
A lovely version of classic baked beans, it's redolent with the smoky flavor of ham and the subtle sweetness of spices and molasses.

CONTEMPORARY RECIPES FOR ALL TYPES OF
DRIED BEANS AND LEGUMES . . .
SPLIT PEAS, BLACK-EYED PEAS, LENTILS,
CHICK-PEAS, WHITE, NAVY, PINTO, KIDNEY, BLACK,
LIMA, AND SOYBEANS

Also by Tamara Holt

BROCCOLI POWER

BEAN POWER

Tamara Holt

INTRODUCTION BY
MARILYNN LARKIN

A LYNN SONBERG BOOK

Published by
Dell Publishing
a division of
Bantam Doubleday Dell Publishing Group, Inc.
1540 Broadway
New York, New York 10036

Research about legumes and human health and nutrition is ongoing and subject to interpretation. Although every effort has been made to include the most up-to-date and accurate information in this book, there can be no guarantee that what we know about this subject won't change with time. The reader should bear in mind that this book should not be used for self-diagnosis or self-treatment and should consult appropriate medical professionals regarding all health issues and before making any major dietary changes.

ISBN: 0-440-21538-2

Published by arrangment with Lynn Sonberg Book Services, 166 East 56 Street, 3-C, New York, NY 10022

Printed in the United States of America

Published simultaneously in Canada

August 1993

10 9 8 7 6 5 4 3 2 1

RAD

Bean Power is gratefully dedicated to my friends and family for their support, advice, and ideas through the development of this book. A special thank you to my mother, Shawn, and Wally for tasting the recipes and giving praise when it was most needed, and Rhea, Suzanna, Michael, and Gordon for listening to me when I was full of beans.

Contents

MAIN DISHES

MAIN DISH SALADS

PASTAS

SALADS

SIDE DISHES

SWEETS

INTRODUCTION

Want to cut your risk of developing cancer? Combat heart disease? Keep your weight under control? Trim your food budget? One important step can set you on the path to all these goals: adding beans to your daily diet.

The American Cancer Society, the National Cancer Institute, the American Heart Association, and other leading health organizations are urging Americans to cut down on total fat intake and eat more high-fiber foods—easy to do when beans are on the menu! The reasons for these recommendations are twofold:

- A high-fat diet appears to play a role in the development of breast, colon, and prostate cancers. Too much dietary fat has also been implicated in heart disease. Of course, a high-fat diet can also make you fat—and obesity itself is a risk factor for a host of ills, including most major cancers, heart disease, high blood pressure, and adult-onset diabetes.

- A high-fiber diet, on the other hand, appears to protect against disease—reducing the risk of cancer, helping prevent heart disease, facilitating weight loss, and maintaining a desirable weight.

Amazingly, including beans at mealtime can help you follow *both* of these important health guidelines. Beans help you reduce the amount of fat in your diet primarily by acting as an alternative source of protein; instead of getting your protein from meat and poultry, which often contain high amounts of saturated animal fat, you can get this important nutrient from beans—which contain only very small amounts (in most cases less than one gram) of vegetable fat.

As far as fiber is concerned, beans in all their forms are *loaded* with this health-promoting nutrient: one cup of cooked kidney beans, for example, contains a whopping *12.2* grams of fiber, while one cup of cooked split peas—also part of the bean family—contains an incredible *16.2* grams of fiber, according to 1992 unpublished data from the U.S. Department of Agriculture, Human Nutrition Information Service. Nutrition experts advise eating between 20 and 30 grams of fiber daily to enjoy protective benefits—which means just a single serving of beans can meet *more than half* of our daily requirement.

In addition to protein and fiber, beans also contain generous amounts of other nutrients vital to good health: carbohydrates, the body's main fuel; B-vitamins, which play a key role in facilitating cell production and the maintenance of skin, eyes, hair, and nails; iron, a mineral essential for healthy blood; and calcium, which helps promote strong bones.

When it comes to versatile, good-tasting, reasonably priced "health" foods, beans are hard to beat! Include beans as part of an overall varied diet low in fat and low to moderate in calories, and you will be taking giant steps on the road to good health.

WHAT IS A BEAN?

Beans are members of the *legume* family, which also includes certain peas, such as split and black-eyed. Technically speaking, legumes are plants that contain pods with seeds inside them. The word "legume" may describe the plant itself or the beans and peas they contain.

Popular members of the legume family include black beans, kidney beans, navy beans, lentils, soybeans, chickpeas (also known as garbanzo beans), and black-eyed peas. These and other legumes are highlighted in the recipes in this book, and are described in more detail later.

A few of the legumes, such as snap beans, mung beans, and fresh (not dry) lima beans, are really considered vegetables, and aren't included in *Bean Power*. While these beans are certainly valuable foods, they are not as rich in the fiber and other nutrients that make true legumes especially healthful.

WHY YOU NEED THIS BOOK

Despite their power-packed nutrient composition, until recently beans weren't accorded the respect they deserve in the American diet. Because they're inexpensive, and because they can cause gas when eaten in excess (more about ways to reduce gas later), we tended to look down our noses at these wholesome and hearty edibles.

No longer. In recent years, our attitude toward beans has been changing for the better, with the growing realization that beans—like vegetables, fruits, and grains—contain nutrients vital for good health and disease prevention.

Actually, we've basically rediscovered what people from diverse parts of the world have known for centuries. In Europe, the Near East, Asia, and Central and South America, people have built their diets around beans and grains for thousands of years. Now Americans are recognizing the nutritional and money-saving wisdom of doing the same.

Recent surveys suggest approximately 10 percent of Americans are eating more beans, vegetables, and grains —and less meat—than ever before. Four out of ten consumers say they have even changed their dining-out habits to reflect nutritional concerns. Not surprisingly, this new direction has prompted a virtual explosion of restaurants and fast-food outlets that serve a wide variety of ethnic, bean-based dishes such as chili, rice, and beans and fajitas.

Quick and Easy Meals

With this book, you can prepare many of the same tasty meals you enjoy when eating out—in minutes, right at home! Are you a chili lover? Try our hearty Two-Bean Chili (p. 51). Roll-Your-Own Fajitas, filled with meat, rice, beans, and salad fixings (p. 55). Or dip into a robust South-of-the-Border Black Bean Dip (p. 29)—the perfect, healthy accompaniment to raw veggies or chips.

Of course, *Bean Power* contains many other delicious recipes as well. In the Soups section, you'll find palate pleasers that do double duty as a first course or a light meal on their own. In a mere fifteen minutes, you can savor a delectable Chick-Pea and Watercress soup (p. 42). In even less time, you can prepare a lovely and wholesome White Bean Soup (p. 37)—and much more.

Main Dishes presents beans in all their glory. Try irresistible Yellow Split Pea Fritters with Roasted Red Pepper Sauce (p. 70); eye-catching, mouth-watering Shrimp and Asparagus with Gingered Bean Sauce (p. 58); or a richly satisfying Lentil Meat Loaf (p. 68).

Main Dish Salads include a delicious eight-minute marvel, Kidney Bean, Chicken, and Mango Salad (p. 93) and a continental favorite, Classic Italian White Bean and Tuna Salad (p. 94).

Pastas and the incredibly versatile bean also give these dishes a creative twist: flavorful Mexican Lasagne (p. 107), for instance, or healthful and tasty Spinach and Chick-Pea Shells (p. 105).

Salads and Side Dishes are next. Imagine immersing your fork in an Orangy Sweet Potato with Red and White Kidney Beans (p. 141) or a taste-tempting Mashed Split Peas and Potatoes (p. 132). Salad starters include a sweet and tangy Fruited Wild Rice and Bean Salad (p. 123) and a Middle East–style Crunchy Curried Yellow Split Pea, Brown Rice, and Apple Salad (p. 125).

Finally, our treats in the Sweets section: scrumptious Raspberry Almond Bean Pie is practically a meal unto itself (p. 151). For a lighter touch, top off your meal with Molasses Bean Soufflé with Lemon-Ginger Sauce (p. 153).

These remarkable dishes and many, many more in *Bean Power* will enrich your menus, tickle your taste buds, and add lots of good nutritional and life-lasting benefits to you and your family's diet in minutes!

BEANS BATTLE DISEASE

Enlisting beans to help fend off disease is one of the smartest dietary moves you can make. Here's a look at beans' exceptional health-promoting properties.

Beans Help Reduce Cancer Risks

Beans play several roles as cancer-fighters. As we've seen, they contain lots of fiber. According to the American Cancer Society, fiber functions in diverse ways that may reduce cancer risk. Fiber dilutes the contents of the colon, thus limiting contact between the lining of the colon and any carcinogens that may be present. Fiber also helps reduce the concentration of carcinogens and other cancer promoters, such as bile acids. And, in contrast to low fiber diets, diets high in fiber tend to be lower in calories and higher in vitamins and minerals, which can also exert a protective effect against cancer.

Beans contain very little fat—another plus in protecting against cancer. Some studies show a correlation between high dietary fat intake and cancers of the breast, colon, and prostate; these studies suggest fat may somehow promote tumor development. Other studies implicate excessive calories (easy to consume on a diet that contains lots of high-fat foods) as the culprit in the development of these and other cancers.

Either way, beans are winners: they're chock-full of nutrients, extremely low in fat, filling and satisfying, and they weigh in at an average of 230 calories per cup, cooked—making only a very modest contribution to your day's total calories.

Beans Help Protect Against Heart Disease

Beans aid in the fight against heart disease by helping to lower blood cholesterol levels and, again, reducing the amount of fat in our diet.

More than one in four Americans suffers from some form of cardiovascular disease, according to the American Heart Association. A major contributing factor to the development of heart disease is a high blood cholesterol level. Studies suggest that the fiber in beans—as well as in fruit, vegetables, and certain grains—can play a role in lowering blood cholesterol levels, thereby reducing the risk of heart disease (for details, see the section on Fiber, p. 9).

As part of an overall healthy diet low to moderate in calories, beans also help prevent heart disease by helping you maintain a desirable weight. Obesity is a major risk factor for heart disease.

Beans Help Manage Diabetes

Beans can play an important role in a diabetic diet because they're high in carbohydrates and fiber—both of which help keep blood sugar on an even keel.

According to the American Diabetes Association (ADA), 55 to 60 percent of a diabetic's calories should come from carbohydrates (the same as everyone else's), with simple carbohydrates (sugar) contributing no more than 5 percent of these calories. The ADA also recommends that a person with diabetes consume 35 to 40 grams of fiber daily—compared with a recommendation of 25 to 30 grams for a nondiabetic person.

Once again, beans fill the bill. As we saw earlier, beans contain large amounts of fiber. And from 60 to 75 percent of beans' calories come from carbohydrate, depending on the type of bean (the remaining calories come mainly from protein). Because of their high fiber and carbohydrate content, beans are now encouraged on a diabetic diet.

Beans Combat Overweight

Beans combat obesity for several reasons. First, they have a low caloric density—meaning you get lots of filling food and nutrition for relatively few calories. Beans' calories come largely from carbohydrates and protein, each of which contains *four* calories per gram. Fat, on the other hand, contains *nine* calories per gram. So foods high in fat are considered calorie *dense:* you get more calories, less satisfaction, and less nutrition per serving.

The high carbohydrate content of beans means that calories from beans are burned up by the body very quickly and converted into usable energy. This contrasts with calories from high-fat foods, which the body tends to store rather than use. There's also some evidence that burning calories from carbohydrates actually causes the body to burn even more calories, setting off a snowball-type effect. We'll explore how this works in more detail later.

The fiber in beans also assists in weight loss and maintenance. Fiber helps you feel "full" and, therefore, you'll be less likely to overeat during a meal (the effect is similar to drinking water before a meal to curb hunger). High-fiber foods also help the dieter because they require more chewing; this forces you to eat more slowly and, in all probability, consume less food than you would if you could simply gulp down your meal.

A CLOSER LOOK AT KEY NUTRIENTS

Fiber, complex carbohydrates, low-fat protein, and certain vitamins and minerals form the foundation of beans' contribution to good health. A closer look at these important nutrients reveals how they perform their nutritional magic.

Fiber

We've seen that the large amounts of fiber contained in beans help combat cancer and heart disease, manage diabetes, and assist in weight control. To gain a better understanding of how this is accomplished, it's important to know some facts about fiber and how it works in the body.

Fiber comes in two main forms: soluble and insoluble. Soluble fiber dissolves easily in water, forming a gummy, gluelike material. Insoluble fiber does not dissolve.

Plant foods contain both types of fiber but, depending on the plant, one type predominates. In beans, it's soluble fiber. The exact mechanism by which beans protect against cancer and heart disease isn't yet known. But it appears that soluble fiber's main health-promoting action is to remove bile acids—substances necessary for the digestion of fat—from the body. The prompt removal of bile acids from the body may help reduce the risk of cancer—particularly cancer of the colon—because when bile acids are eliminated they take potential carcinogens with them.

With respect to soluble fiber's role in helping to prevent heart disease, the picture is somewhat more complicated: The elimination of bile acids that become entangled in the gummy web of soluble fiber prompts the body to produce more bile acids for later use in fat digestion.

Cholesterol contains some of the chemical substances needed to produce bile acids. So, in order to produce more bile acids, the body must first remove some of the circulating cholesterol from the blood. The result: less cholesterol circulating in the blood—and a lowered risk of heart disease.

Dietary Fiber Content of Beans and Legumes	
	grams per ¹/₂ cup, cooked
Black beans	7.5
Black-eyed peas	4.6
Chick-peas	6.2
Kidney beans	6.1
Lentils	7.8
Lima beans	6.6
Navy beans	4.6
Pinto beans	7.3
Soybeans	5.2
Split peas	8.1
White beans	5.7

Complex Carbohydrates

Carbohydrates play a role in weight reduction and regulation of blood sugar levels. But not all carbohydrates are created equal.

Like fiber, carbohydrates come in two main forms: simple carbohydrates, found largely in table sugar and candy; and complex carbohydrates, found in beans and other starchy, high-fiber foods. Both forms are eventually broken down into glucose, the body's main fuel. So why choose complex carbohydrates over the simple ones?

For several good reasons. First, foods high in complex carbohydrates—beans, vegetables, fruits, grains—are also rich in other important vitamins and minerals necessary for health. Simple carbohydrate foods such as candy and cookies generally contain little in the way of nutrients.

As we've seen, complex carbohydrates have a low caloric density, meaning you get lots of nutrition—and a feeling of "fullness"—for relatively few calories. Therefore, complex carbohydrates are a boon for weight control. Simple carbohydrates, like fats, tend to be calorie dense: even small servings of simple carbohydrates contain relatively high amounts of calories and little else. For example, a half-cup serving of cooked beans—with its complex carbohydrates, fiber, protein, vitamins, and minerals—contains about the same number of calories as a roll of candy mints.

There are additional benefits to including plenty of complex carbohydrates in your diet. They help keep blood sugar on an even keel, which is important for diabetics and nondiabetics alike. A dramatic rise in blood sugar levels, which can occur after you eat a food high in simple carbohydrates, is generally followed by a precipitous *drop* in blood sugar levels. This results in energy highs and lows that can interfere with functioning. Complex carbohydrates, on the other hand, allow a relatively steady trickle of glucose into the blood after a meal, because it takes the body time to break them down and digest them.

The way in which carbohydrates are digested by the body also has a beneficial result. The body appears to expend more calories when digesting carbohydrates than it does in the digestion of fat. Therefore, carbohydrate foods are said to have a greater *thermic effect*—they cause more calories to be burned after eating—than high fat foods. It seems that 25 percent of excess carbohydrate calories are used up in the digestion and conversion of carbohydrates to body fat, whereas almost all of the excess fat calories we consume are immediately stored as body fat. So by eating foods high in carbohydrates—especially the complex kind—you actually give your body fewer calories to convert into fat.

Some studies suggest that the thermic effect stimulates the body to *continue* burning carbohydrates for as long as two hours after you've eaten a high-carbohydrate meal. No such effect occurs after consumption of a high-fat meal.

Protein

Protein, like oxygen, is essential to the proper functioning of every cell in the body. The brain, muscles, skin, hair, nails, and tissues that hold the body together are all made primarily of protein—and beans are an excellent source of this vital nutrient.

Protein, like fiber and carbohydrates, comes in two main forms: complete protein, found in animal foods such as meat, poultry, fish, and dairy products—and incomplete protein, found in beans, grains, and other plant foods. The amount and type of *amino acids* the protein contains determine whether it is complete or incomplete.

Amino acids are divided into two types: essential amino acids, which must be provided by the diet, and nonessential amino acids, which are produced by the body (but may also come from diet). Animal foods contain all the essential amino acids, and are therefore complete. Plant foods such as beans are deficient in one or more essential amino acids. Fortunately, however, all plant foods are not low in the same amino acids. By combining plant foods that are low in different essential amino acids, you can obtain adequate amounts of complete protein even if you don't eat animal foods. Two proteins that compensate for each other's deficiencies in this way are called *complementary proteins.*

Many of the recipes in this book include complementary proteins, such as the black-eyed peas and rice in Herbed Hoppin' John (p. 147) and the Brown Rice and Red Bean Pilaf (p. 145).

B Vitamins

Adequate amounts of B vitamins are vital for a strong immune system, high energy, healthy skin, hair, and nails, and the production of healthy blood cells. Beans are an excellent source of all the B vitamins (except vitamin B_{12}, which is only present in animal foods). In addition to fiber, complex carbohydrates, and protein, the B vitamins are a major nutritional plus for beans.

Iron

Beans are also an excellent source of iron, with anywhere from 3 to 6 milligrams per cup, cooked, depending on the variety of bean. Iron is vital for healthy red blood cells, and adequate amounts are needed to avoid the debilitating effects of iron-deficiency anemia.

There are two types of dietary iron: *heme* iron, the form found in animal foods, and *nonheme* iron, found in beans and other plant foods. Nonheme iron is not as easily absorbed by the body as heme iron. However, eating foods that contain nonheme iron with foods that contain vitamin C (such as fruits and vegetables), or with an animal food, makes nonheme iron more available. Most of the recipes in this book feature beans in combination with fruits or vegetables, meat, poultry, or fish.

Calcium

Calcium is vital for healthy bones and teeth, and also plays a role in keeping our immune system sound. Beans are a good source of calcium, providing between 50 and 130 milligrams per cup, depending on the type of bean. Soybeans contain the highest amounts of calcium among the members of the legume family.

OVERCOMING "GASSINESS"

Gassiness, technically known as flatulence, is a consequence of the digestion of certain types of sugars, called *oligosaccharides*, contained in beans. Although they can't be eliminated entirely, the amount of oligosaccharides in beans can be reduced during preparation and cooking.

Most food substances are digested in the stomach and small intestine, and remaining indigestible substances are sent into the large intestine for removal from the body. But the oligosaccharides in beans aren't digested in the stomach or small intestine; instead, they arrive intact in the large intestine, where they are digested by bacteria. The digestion process causes the beans to ferment, producing gas.

During preparation, you can reduce the amount of oligosaccharides in beans—and thereby reduce their gas-causing potential—by discarding the water you've used to soak beans and replacing that water with 3 or 4 cups of fresh water before cooking. If you're using shortcut methods of preparation—bringing cooking water to a boil and dropping legumes into the boiling water, or using a pressure cooker—then discard the cooking water from the pot or pressure cooker halfway through and resume cooking with fresh water. A pinch of baking soda to the cooking water will also reduce the gassiness sometimes caused by beans. Commercial preparations such as Beano to improve bean digestion may also be purchased at health food stores.

GETTING TO KNOW BEANS

Legumes are probably the oldest form of food known to mankind, and many different varieties are grown around the world. Here's a look at the more popular beans and peas in the American diet, which are included in *Bean Power*.

Black Beans

These sweet-tasting beans are thick and hearty—perfect for soups and salads. For a delicious, south-of-the-border treat, try our Black Bean Soup (p. 47) or our Black Bean, Avocado, and Yellow Rice Salad (p. 91).

Black-eyed Peas

These tasty peas—white with a black spot on the side—are the main ingredient of the popular dish, Herbed Hoppin' John (p. 147). One of several varieties of cowpeas, black-eyed peas thrive in a warm climate and are an important food throughout the Southern states.

Chick-Peas (Garbanzos)

These yellow peas have a hazelnut shape and size, and a delicate, nutty flavor. They're popular in Middle Eastern–style dishes, such as Hummus (p. 33) and Moroccan-style Chick-Pea and Vegetable Couscous Casserole (p. 80).

Kidney Beans

These versatile red or white kidney-shaped beans have a firm skin, but are tender and sweet inside. They're the main ingredient in many Mexican dishes, including our Vegetable Bean Enchiladas (p. 53) and Refried Beans (p. 129)

Lentils

These tan or red, small disk-shape beans are terrific for soups, salads, and dishes that require a thick, "meaty" texture. Try our Lentil Soup (p. 43), Lentil Meat Loaf (p. 68), or Lentil and Orange Salad (p. 122).

Lima Beans

Lima beans have the unusual distinction of being both a bean (in its dried, white form) and a vegetable (when fresh and green). They're native to the Americas and were grown by the Indians for centuries before the arrival of Columbus. The name "Lima" comes from the city of Lima, capital of Peru, where early explorers from Europe first discovered this bean.

For an unusual side dish, try our Lima Beans with Lemon and Poppy Seeds (p. 135).

Navy Beans

Navy beans are white with an oval shape and have a sweet, delicate flavor. They're popular baked, and in salads and casseroles. Try our Light-style Baked Beans with Ham (p. 74), White Bean and Watercress Salad with Tomato Dressing (p. 119), or Pasta and Vegetables with Cheesy White Bean Sauce (p. 103).

Pinto Beans

These beige or speckled beans have a delicate flavor. Like the kidney bean, they're a favorite ingredient in chilis and salads. Try our Curried Pinto Bean Dip (p. 30) and our Pinto Bean Salad with Ham (p. 116).

Soybeans

Soybeans have a delicate flavor, and are often used as a meat substitute. Of all the legumes, they have the most complete protein—similar to the protein found in meat. Try our hearty Two-Bean Chili (p. 51), or crunchy Soybean Granola (p. 157) at breakfast or snack time.

Split Peas

These yellow or green peas complement just about any type of dish, including our Split Pea and Spinach Soup (p. 39) and our Crunchy Curried Yellow Split Pea, Brown Rice, and Apple Salad (p. 125).

BUYING GUIDE

Packaged dried beans provide a world of healthful nutrients for just pennies per serving. Even canned beans,
which cost more per serving than dried beans, are a terrific nutritional bargain. You get ample amounts of protein, fiber, vitamins, and minerals for a fraction of the
cost of animal foods. And what you *don't* get counts, too—
no cholesterol, and very small amounts of fat.

- For best taste and nutrition, buy beans as soon as possi-
  ble after packaging. Shop in stores that have a rapid
  turnover of goods; try different outlets and brands.

- Look for firm, clean beans with no visible dirt or small
  stones.

- Beans should be similar in size and color; otherwise,
  they will cook unevenly.

- Make sure bags are strong and well sealed, with no
  punctures or openings.

- If buying beans loose from a bin, sift through and se-
  lect beans with a fresh appearance. Avoid beans with
  tiny pinholes, which can be a sign of bug infestation.

- If buying canned beans, check the freshness date.

STORAGE TIPS

- Store beans in their plastic bags until ready for use.
  After opening, transfer remaining beans to glass jars
  with tight-fitting lids and store in a cool, dry place.

- Never mix different types of beans or older beans with new ones; they all require different soaking and cooking times.

- Beans can be stored for years, but are best if used within six to nine months of purchase.

- Keep cooked beans tightly covered in the refrigerator for use within five days.

Ready for an adventure in the delightful world of bean cookery? Turn the page to learn how to prepare beans— and cook them to perfection!

BEAN BASICS

HOW TO SOAK AND COOK DRIED BEANS

Soaking and cooking dried beans is neither difficult nor complicated. Use either soaking method outlined below and cook the beans for the necessary amount of time for that particular bean. Lentils, split peas, and black-eyed peas do not need to be soaked, but other beans do. Many recipes can be made with canned beans, however I generally prefer soaked dried beans unless I'm in a real hurry. If you choose to use canned beans, be sure to rinse and drain them before using them in the recipe.

Quick-Soaking Method:
1. Rinse and pick over dried beans. Place beans and three times their volume of hot water in a saucepan. Bring the beans to a boil and boil for 2 minutes.

2. Remove the saucepan from heat and allow the beans to soak for 1 hour. Drain and rinse the beans before cooking.

Traditional Soaking Method:
1. Rinse and pick over dried beans. Place beans and three times their volume of hot water in a bowl.

2. Allow beans to soak for 4 hours or overnight. They will not absorb much more water than can be absorbed in 4 hours, but you may soak longer for convenience. (Soybeans will need the full 12 hours of soaking.) Change the soaking water a few times during soaking. This will help to break down the indigestible sugars that can lead to flatulence.

3. Drain and rinse the beans before cooking.

How to Cook Beans:
Cooking time:

Adzuki	1–1$^1/_2$ hours
Black Beans	1$^1/_2$ hours
Black-Eyed Peas	1 hour
Cannelini (White Kidney) Beans	1 hour
Chick-Peas	2–2$^1/_2$ hours
Great Northern Beans	1$^1/_2$ hours
Kidney (red) Beans	1$^1/_2$ hours
Lentils	30–35 minutes
Lima Beans	1–1$^1/_2$ hours
Navy Beans	2 hours
Pigeon Peas	30 minutes
Pink Beans	1–1$^1/_2$ hours
Pinto Beans	1–1$^1/_2$ hours
Red Beans	1–1$^1/_2$ hours
Small White Beans	2 hours
Split Peas	30 minutes
Soybeans	3–3$^1/_2$ hours

Yield: 1 pound dry beans = 2 cups dry = 5–6 cups cooked

Cooking Beans:

1. Place soaked beans in a large saucepan. Cover with three times their volume of water. Add herbs or spices as desired. Do not add salt or acidic ingredients such as vinegar, tomatoes, or juice, which substantially slow the cooking. Add these ingredients when the beans are just tender.

2. Bring to a boil, lower heat, and simmer gently, stirring occasionally until tender. Do not boil the beans or their skins will break. Cooking times vary with the type

of beans used, but may also vary with the age of the
beans. Beans are done when they can be easily mashed
between two fingers, or with a fork. Always test a few
beans in case they are unevenly cooked.

3. Rinse and drain.

HOW TO SPROUT BEANS

Adzuki, lentils, soybeans, and even chick-peas can be
sprouted. Try sprouting with all the different varieties.

Yield: 2 to 3 tablespoons dry beans = $1^1/_2$ cups sprouts

1. Soak beans by traditional method (see p. 23). Drain.

2. Place the beans in a glass jar. Cover the jar with a
   double layer of cheesecloth, secured with a rubber
   band.

3. Rinse the beans twice daily, for 4 or 5 days, draining
   water through the cheesecloth. Be sure to drain the
   beans well each time. Remove the unsprouted beans
   and serve sprouts with or as a salad, with your favorite
   dressing.

DIPS AND SPREADS

SOUTH-OF-THE-BORDER BLACK BEAN DIP

Try this healthy dip at your next party. Serve it with fresh salsa and salt-free tortilla chips.

Preparation time: 2 minutes
Cooking time: 1 minute
Makes 1 cup

> 2 teaspoons ground cumin
> 2 cups cooked black beans
> 2 tablespoons chopped green bell pepper
> 2 tablespoons chopped red bell pepper
> 1 tablespoon olive oil
> 2 teaspoons cider vinegar
> 1 tablespoon minced jalapeño pepper
> Freshly ground black pepper
> Salt, to taste

1. In a small skillet, heat cumin over very low flame, just until fragrant, about 1 minute.

2. Combine cumin and remaining ingredients in a food processor. Process until smooth. Serve with tortilla chips.

CURRIED PINTO BEAN DIP

Serve this dip with crudités or try stuffing it in the whites of hard-cooked eggs for an interesting appetizer. One cup of the dip will fill about 16 egg-white halves.

Preparation time: 3 minutes
Cooking time: 1 minute
Makes 1 cup

  1 tablespoon curry powder
  ¹/₄ teaspoon ground cinnamon
  ¹/₂ teaspoon powdered turmeric
  2 cups cooked pinto beans
  2 tablespoons cider vinegar
  1 tablespoon vegetable oil
  ¹/₂ teaspoon grated orange zest
  Salt, to taste

1. In a small skillet, heat curry powder, cinnamon, and turmeric over very low flame, just until fragrant, about 1 minute.

2. Combine pinto beans, vinegar, oil, orange zest, and salt in a food processor. Add spices. Process until smooth. Serve with fresh vegetables.

GINGERED WHITE BEAN DIP

This is a perfect dip for a summer gathering. Serve it with fresh, crisp vegetable sticks.

Preparation time: 5 minutes
Cooking time: None
Makes 1 cup

2 cups cooked white beans
1 tablespoon grated ginger
4 teaspoons extra-virgin olive oil
1 tablespoon honey
1 tablespoon cider vinegar
$1/2$ teaspoon mustard powder
Pinch white pepper
Salt, to taste
Water
2 teaspoons chopped chives

1. Combine beans, ginger, oil, honey, vinegar, mustard powder, white pepper, and salt in a food processor. Process until smooth, adding water tablespoon by tablespoon, as necessary.

2. Stir in chives and serve with crisp vegetable sticks.

LENTIL AND ONION COMPOTE

This wonderful, naturally sweet spread is delicious on crusty French bread. Serve it as an hors d'oeuvre, an appetizer, or with lunch.

Preparation time: 5 minutes
Cooking time: 65 to 70 minutes
Makes 1¼ cups

> 2 cups diced onions
> 1 tablespoon olive oil
> 1 cup, plus 2 tablespoons water
> 1 cup cooked lentils
> 2 tablespoons sherry
> ½ teaspoon salt, or to taste
> ½ teaspoon freshly ground black pepper

1. In a medium heavy-bottom saucepan, combine onion, oil, and 2 tablespoons water. Cook over medium heat, stirring occasionally, until onion is just golden, 10 to 15 minutes.

2. Add lentils and remaining water, cover, and cook over very low heat for 1 hour, stirring occasionally.

3. Stir in sherry, salt, and pepper and cook uncovered until compote is thick.

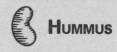 # HUMMUS

Serve this traditional Middle Eastern dip with toasted whole wheat pita triangles. Tahini paste should be available in the Oriental foods section of your supermarket or at the health food store.

Preparation time: 5 minutes
Cooking time: None
Makes 1¹/₂ cups

> 2 cups cooked chick-peas
> ³/₄ cup lemon juice
> ¹/₃ cup tahini (sesame seed) paste
> 3 cloves garlic, chopped
> ¹/₂ teaspoon salt, or to taste

1. Combine all ingredients in a food processor. Process until smooth or to desired consistency.

SOUPS

WHITE BEAN SOUP

This is a perfect, pure white bean soup. Purée more or less of the beans to taste.

Preparation time: 2 minutes
Cooking time: 10 minutes
Serves 6

   3 tablespoons extra-virgin olive oil
   2 cloves garlic, minced
   5¹/₂ cups cooked white beans, any variety
   3 tablespoons chopped parsley
   ¹/₂ teaspoon freshly ground black pepper
   1¹/₂ cups chicken stock, reduced-sodium chicken
      broth, water or broth/water combination
   Salt, to taste

Garnish:

   2 tablespoons finely chopped parsley
   1 teaspoon grated lemon zest,
   ¹/₄ teaspoon freshly ground black pepper

1. In a large (12-inch) nonstick skillet or saucepan, heat oil over medium flame. Add garlic and cook, stirring until tender. Add beans, parsley, and pepper. Stir to coat, add stock and salt, cover, and simmer for 10 minutes. Cool slightly.

(*Continued on next page*)

2. Transfer 1½ cups of the beans to a food processor. Process until smooth and return to skillet. Stir soup and heat through.

3. To prepare garnish: Combine parsley, lemon zest, and pepper. Ladle soup into bowls and sprinkle with garnish.

SPLIT PEA AND SPINACH SOUP

I have been making this soup for years and have no idea where the recipe originally came from. It's one of my all time favorites for a winter lunch.

Preparation time: 3 minutes
Cooking time: 2 to 2¹/₂ hours
Serves 6

2 tablespoons vegetable oil
1 cup chopped onion
1 clove garlic, minced
1 tablespoon whole mustard seeds
1¹/₂ teaspoons powdered turmeric
1 pound dried split peas
5 cups chicken stock, reduced-sodium chicken broth,
    water or a stock/water combination
5 cups water
¹/₂ teaspoon salt
1 10-ounce package frozen chopped spinach,
    defrosted and drained
¹/₄ cup lemon juice, or to taste
Salt, to taste
Freshly ground black pepper, to taste

1. In a large (4-quart) wide saucepan, heat oil over medium flame. Add onion, garlic, mustard seeds, and turmeric. Cook, stirring until onions are tender and mustard seeds begin to pop.

(Continued on next page)

2. Stir in peas, stock, water, and salt. Bring mixture to a boil, reduce heat and simmer, uncovered, stirring occasionally, until peas have disintegrated, 2 to 2$^1/_2$ hours.

3. Add spinach and lemon juice, season with salt and pepper, heat through, and serve.

PASTA E FAGIOLI

This is a light and colorful version of the classic Italian soup.

Preparation time: 10 minutes
Cooking time: 15 minutes
Serves 6

4 cups chicken stock or reduced-sodium chicken broth
2 cups water
1 cup small pasta, such as ditalini
2 cups cooked kidney beans
2 ounces fresh green beans, cut in $1/2$-inch pieces
1 cup tomato, seeded and diced
$1/2$ cup corn kernels
$1/2$ cup finely diced carrot
$1/4$ cup chopped fresh dill
1 tablespoon white vinegar
Salt, to taste
Freshly ground black pepper, to taste

1. In a large saucepan, combine broth and water. Bring to a boil. Add pasta and cook for 5 minutes.

2. Add kidney and green beans, tomato, corn kernels, and carrot, and simmer until pasta is tender. Stir in dill and vinegar and add salt and pepper to taste.

CHICK-PEA AND WATERCRESS SOUP

If you make this soup with canned chick-peas it's a snap! It is also a very impressive-tasting first course or light meal.

Preparation time: 10 minutes
Cooking time: 5 minutes
Serves 6

3 cups chopped onion
3 teaspoons vegetable oil
9 cups cooked chick-peas
3 teaspoons fresh or $^1/_4$ teaspoon dried sage
$^3/_4$ teaspoon freshly ground black pepper
9 cups chicken stock or reduced-sodium chicken broth
6 tablespoons lemon juice
6 cups packed, coarsely chopped watercress
9 tablespoons chopped parsley

1. In a medium saucepan, heat oil over medium flame. Add onion and cook, stirring, until tender. Add chick-peas, sage, and pepper. Toss to coat.

2. Add stock and lemon juice and heat mixture just to boiling. Remove from heat, and cool slightly. Transfer mixture to a food processor and process until smooth.

3. Return chick-pea mixture to saucepan. Add watercress and parsley and heat until watercress is just wilted. Serve promptly.

LENTIL SOUP

This is a wonderful classic lentil soup. Use stock for a rich flavor, water or vegetable stock for a lighter touch.

Preparation time: 10 minutes
Cooking time: 45 to 50 minutes
Serves 8 to 10

3 tablespoons olive oil
1 cup chopped onion
1 cup chopped carrot
1 cup finely chopped celery
4 cloves garlic, minced
1/4 cup chopped parsley
1 teaspoon dried thyme
1/4 teaspoon ground cumin
1 bay leaf
2 cups dried lentils
4 cups chicken or beef stock, reduced-sodium
    chicken or beef broth or water
4 cups water
Tabasco or other hot sauce, to taste
Salt, to taste
Lemon or lime wedges

1. Heat oil in a large (4 to 6 quart) saucepan over medium-low flame. Add onions and cook, stirring, until tender. Add carrots, celery, and garlic and cook until golden, about 5 minutes.

(Continued on next page)

2. Stir lentils, parsley, thyme, cumin, and bay leaf into onion mixture until well coated. Add stock and bring mixture to a boil. Reduce heat and gently simmer soup until lentils are soft, 35 to 45 minutes. Cool slightly.

3. Remove bay leaf and discard. Transfer 2 cups of lentils to a food processor. Process until smooth and return to saucepan. Heat soup through and season with Tabasco and salt. Garnish with lemon or lime wedges.

MINESTRONE

Minestrone literally means "big soup." Serve this one with a thick slice of multigrain bread.

Preparation time: 10 minutes
Cooking time: 45 minutes
Serves 6

2 tablespoons olive oil
1 cup thinly sliced onion
4 cloves garlic, minced
$^3/_4$ cup diced carrots
$^3/_4$ cup diced celery
1 14-ounce can Italian plum tomatoes, diced, including juice
$2^1/_2$ cups chicken or beef stock, reduced-sodium chicken or beef broth, water or broth/water combination
$1^1/_2$ cups shredded red cabbage
3 tablespoons chopped fresh basil
3 tablespoons chopped fresh parsley
$^3/_4$ teaspoon dried thyme
$^3/_4$ teaspoon dried oregano
3 cups cooked pinto, navy or Great Northern beans
$2^1/_2$ cups diced zucchini
Salt, to taste
Grated Parmesan cheese
Freshly ground black pepper, to taste

1. Heat oil in a large (4-quart) saucepan over medium flame. Add onions and cook, stirring until tender. Add

garlic, carrots, and celery and cook until onions are golden.

2. Stir in tomatoes, stock, cabbage, basil, parsley, thyme, and oregano. Bring to a boil, reduce heat and simmer for 30 minutes, stirring occasionally.

3. Add beans and zucchini and simmer for 15 minutes. Add salt to taste. Serve with grated Parmesan cheese and freshly ground black pepper.

Black Bean Soup

Welcome to South America! This light version of Black Bean Soup leaves out the fat of the traditional ham bone or salt pork. But you can serve it with just a sprinkle of chopped ham to give a little of that smoky pork flavor.

Preparation time: 5 minutes
Cooking time: 1¹/₂ to 2 hours
Serves 6 to 7

2 tablespoons olive oil
¹/₂ cup chopped onion
¹/₂ cup chopped red bell pepper
¹/₂ cup chopped green bell pepper
2 cloves garlic, minced
1 small jalapeño pepper
1 teaspoon ground cumin
1 teaspoon oregano
Pinch ground cloves
1 pound dried black beans, soaked
6 cups beef stock or reduced-sodium beef broth
¹/₂ cup dry sherry
1 teaspoon reduced-sodium soy sauce, or to taste

1. In a large (4-quart) saucepan, heat oil, onions, peppers, and garlic over medium flame. Cook, stirring, until onions are tender. Add cumin, oregano, and cloves and cook for 2 minutes.

2. Stir in beans and stock. Bring mixture to a boil, reduce heat, and simmer, uncovered, until beans are very soft. Add sherry and soy sauce and simmer for 20 minutes.

MINTED SPLIT AND FRESH PEA SOUP

I have been making a fresh pea soup for years, but here is a protein-rich version using split peas, as well. This fresh and delicious soup can be served hot, but is especially wonderful served chilled in the summer.

Preparation time: 3 minutes
Cooking time: 35 to 40 minutes
Serves 4 to 5

3/4 cup dried split peas
3 cups water
1 10-ounce package frozen peas, thawed
3 tablespoons chopped fresh mint
1/2 teaspoon salt, or to taste
Pinch freshly ground black pepper

1. Place split peas and water in a saucepan over medium heat. Simmer until tender, about 30 minutes. Add frozen peas and continue simmering until they are cooked, 6 to 7 minutes. Cool slightly.

2. Place peas, water, mint, salt, and pepper in a food processor. Process until smooth. Serve hot or chill and serve.

MAIN DISHES

Two-Bean Chili

If chili served over rice is the perfect winter meal, could chili made with soybeans be more than perfect? Soybeans have the highest protein content of any bean. Here's to your health!

Preparation time: 10 minutes
Cooking time: 50 minutes
Serves 8

2 tablespoons vegetable oil
1 cup chopped onion
3 cloves garlic, minced
1 cup diced carrot
1 1/2 tablespoons chili powder
1 teaspoon ground cumin
1/2 teaspoon cayenne pepper
1 teaspoon ground allspice
2 28-ounce cans plum tomatoes, including juice
3 cups cooked soybeans, chopped in a food
   processor
2 cups cooked kidney beans
2 teaspoons dijon mustard
1 teaspoon salt, or to taste
Freshly ground pepper, to taste

1. In a large saucepan, heat oil over medium flame. Add onion and cook, stirring, until translucent. Add garlic and carrot and continue cooking until onions are

golden. Stir in chili powder, cumin, cayenne, and all-spice and cook for 1 minute.

2. Stir in tomatoes and simmer for five minutes, breaking up the whole tomatoes with a spoon. Stir in beans and continue cooking until thickened, about 45 minutes.

3. Stir in mustard and season to taste with salt and pepper. Serve with chopped onion and a dollop of low-fat yogurt.

Vegetable Bean Enchiladas

These enchiladas are simply delicious! Light, fresh tasting and so easy to make, serve them with rice for a great meal.

Preparation time: 15 minutes
Cooking time: 40 to 45 minutes
Serves 4 to 6

1 28-ounce can crushed tomatoes
1¹/₂ teaspoon chili powder
1 teaspoon ground cumin
¹/₃ cup water
1 tablespoon vegetable or olive oil
1 cup diced onion
2 cloves garlic, minced
1 cup diced red bell pepper
1 cup diced green bell pepper
2 cups chopped broccoli, steamed to crisp-tender
1 cup diced tomatoes, juice reserved
Salt, to taste
Freshly ground black pepper, to taste
10 flour tortillas
1 recipe refried beans (see p. 129)
1 cup shredded reduced-fat cheddar cheese

1. Preheat oven to 375°F. In a small saucepan, combine crushed tomatoes, water, chili powder, and cumin. Bring to a boil, reduce heat, cover, and simmer for 10 minutes. Set aside. (*Continued on next page*)

2. Meanwhile, heat oil in a large nonstick skillet, over medium flame. Add onion and cook, stirring until tender, about 3 minutes. Add peppers, broccoli, and garlic and continue cooking until peppers are tender, another 5 minutes. Add tomatoes and reserved juice and $1/4$ cup water, cover and cook for 4 minutes.

3. Divide the refried beans and spread evenly down the center of each of the 10 tortillas. Top each with some of the vegetable mixture, and sprinkle with 1 tablespoon of cheese.

4. Roll enchiladas and place, seam side down, side by side in a shallow baking dish. Leave $1/2$ inch between each. Top with sauce and sprinkle with remaining cheese.

5. Bake for 30 minutes. Serve with rice.

ROLL-YOUR-OWN FAJITAS

Perfect for an easy and healthy party! Serve meat, rice and beans, vegetables, lettuce, sauce, and tortillas on separate serving platters and let everyone roll their own. For a lighter choice, try replacing the traditional tortillas with lettuce leaves!

Preparation time: 15 minutes, plus marination time
Cooking time: 30 minutes
Serves 7 to 8

14 to 16 flour tortillas
1¹/₂ pounds flank steak or boneless chicken breasts
¹/₄ head iceberg lettuce, finely shredded

Marinade:

¹/₄ cup lime juice
2 tablespoons grated ginger
1 tablespoon olive oil
4 dashes Tabasco sauce

Sauce:

2 cups plain low-fat yogurt
¹/₂ cup chopped cilantro
2 cloves garlic, minced

Rice and beans:

3 cups cooked black beans
3 cups cooked brown rice

(*Continued on next page*)

    1 tablespoon olive oil
    1 large onion, chopped
    2 cloves garlic, minced
    1 teaspoon ground cumin
    1¹/₂ teaspoons chili powder
    1 35-ounce can tomatoes, drained and coarsely
        chopped

Vegetables:

    1¹/₂ tablespoons olive oil
    2 red peppers, cored and cut in long strips
    2 green peppers, cored and cut in long strips
    2 medium zucchini, sliced ¹/₄-inch thick
    2 yellow squash, sliced ¹/₄-inch thick
    Salt, to taste
    Freshly ground black pepper, to taste

1. Place beef or chicken in a shallow nonmetal baking
   dish. Mix together marinade ingredients and pour
   over meat. Leave for 1 hour.

2. Mix together sauce ingredients. Refrigerate until
   needed.

3. To prepare rice and beans: Heat 1 tablespoon oil in a
   heavy-bottom, 4-quart saucepan over medium flame.
   Add onions and cook until translucent, stirring frequently. Add garlic and spices and cook for 1 minute,
   stirring constantly.

4. Add tomatoes, and simmer for 3 minutes. Add rice and
   beans. Stir. Add pepper and salt to taste. Set aside.

5. To prepare vegetables: Heat $1^{1}/_{2}$ tablespoons of oil in a large skillet. Add vegetables and sauté until tender. Season with salt and pepper to taste.

6. Place steak or chicken on a broiler rack. Broil one side until nicely browned. Turn meat, brush with marinade, and continue cooking. Chicken should be cooked through, about 8 minutes. Allow meat to rest for 2 minutes before cutting.

7. Slice meat on a strong diagonal. Arrange platters on the table and instruct your guests to roll a little bit of everything in their tortillas and eat them with their hands.

SHRIMP AND ASPARAGUS WITH GINGERED BEAN SAUCE

Beans take on other flavors beautifully. Here, shrimp and asparagus are tossed with a lovely bean sauce enhanced with sweet and pungent flavors.

Preparation time: 5 minutes
Cooking time: 5 minutes
Serves 4

    1 pound asparagus, stems trimmed and peeled, cut
        into 2-inch lengths
    2 cups cooked Great Northern beans
    1 tablespoon, plus 1 teaspoon grated ginger
    1 tablespoon cider vinegar
    1 tablespoon orange juice
    1/4 teaspoon freshly ground black pepper
    Pinch nutmeg
    Salt, to taste
    1 tablespoon olive oil
    1 pound large shrimp, peeled and deveined
    2 tablespoons slivered fresh basil leaves

1. Blanch asparagus in boiling water until crisp-tender, about 2 minutes.

2. In a food processor, combine beans, 1 tablespoon ginger, vinegar, orange juice, pepper, nutmeg, and salt. Process until smooth, adding more orange juice, tablespoon by tablespoon, as necessary until sauce reaches desired consistency. Set aside.

3. In a large nonstick skillet, heat oil and 1 teaspoon ginger, over medium-high flame. Add shrimp and asparagus and cook for 1 minute. Quickly add white bean purée and toss with shrimp and asparagus. Cook until shrimp turn pink. Toss with basil and serve with brown rice.

WHITE BEAN RISOTTO WITH SHRIMP

This dish is an interesting twist on the classic risotto. It uses regular long-grain rice instead of short-grain arborio and does not have to be constantly stirred. The best surprise, however, is the addition of the beans which are a wonderful complement, especially in terms of nutrition.

Preparation time: 5 minutes
Cooking time: 25 to 30 minutes
Serves 5 to 6

> $3^1/_2$ cups chicken stock or reduced-sodium chicken broth
> 2 teaspoons olive oil
> $^1/_4$ cup chopped onion
> 1 cup long grain white rice
> 2 cups cooked white beans
> 3 tablespoons lemon juice
> 2 teaspoons lemon zest
> 1 pound shrimp, cleaned and peeled
> 1 cup packed watercress leaves
> 1 teaspoon fresh thyme leaves
> Freshly ground black pepper, to taste

1. Heat broth to boiling. Lower heat and simmer.

2. In a large saucepan, combine oil and onion and cook until onion is tender. Add rice and stir to coat.

3. Add 1 cup of the hot broth, stir, cover, and simmer over a very low heat for 5 minutes. Add 1 more cup of

broth and beans, stir, cover, and simmer for another 10 minutes.

4. Add $1/2$ cup broth, lemon juice, and zest. Cook, stirring until broth is absorbed. Continue stirring and adding broth, $1/2$ cup at a time, making sure that liquid is absorbed between each addition, until rice is just tender. If you run out of stock, continue cooking with water.

5. Stir in shrimp, watercress, thyme, and pepper and cook, stirring, until the shrimp are pink. Serve promptly.

BROILED SALMON ON LEMONY WHITE BEAN PURÉE

This bean purée is heavenly. It can be served as a side dish or topped with a perfectly cooked piece of fish, as in this recipe.

Preparation time: 10 minutes, plus marination time
Cooking time: 10 to 15 minutes
Serves 4

    4 salmon fillets, about $^1/_3$ pound each
    1 tablespoon chopped parsley, for garnish

Marinade:

    $^1/_2$ cup white wine
    2 tablespoons olive oil
    2 tablespoons lemon juice
    $^1/_2$ teaspoon salt
    $^1/_2$ teaspoon dried thyme
    $^1/_4$ teaspoon dried sage
    $^1/_4$ teaspoon dried basil
    1 tablespoon chopped parsley

Bean purée:

    3 cups cooked cannelini beans
    $^1/_4$ cup lemon juice
    1 tablespoon lemon zest
    2 teaspoons butter, melted
    2 teaspoons vegetable or extra-virgin olive oil

Salt, to taste
$^1/_2$ teaspoon freshly ground black pepper

1. Place fish in a shallow, nonmetal baking dish. Whisk together the marinade ingredients. Pour over fish and allow it to marinate for 1 to 2 hours.

2. Broil fish until lightly browned on top, turn, and cook it until fork-tender, 10 to 15 minutes, depending on thickness.

3. Meanwhile, place beans, lemon juice and zest, butter, oil, salt, and pepper in a food processor. Purée until smooth.

4. Divide purée on individual serving plates. Place fish on top of purée and spoon remaining juices over it. Sprinkle with fresh chopped parsley. Serve promptly.

GINGERED CHICKEN AND CHICK-PEA CURRY

The chick-pea is the most common legume in Indian cuisine. Here is a very simple chicken curry.

Preparation time: 5 minutes
Cooking time: 70 to 75 minutes
Serves 4

3 cloves garlic, minced
1-inch cube ginger, peeled and diced
3 tablespoons water
2 tablespoons vegetable oil
¹/₂ cup chopped onion
1 tablespoon curry powder
1 pound skinned and boned chicken breasts, diced
1 tablespoon flour
3 cups chicken stock or reduced-sodium chicken broth
3 cups cooked chick-peas
¹/₂ cup tomato, peeled, seeded, and diced
3 tablespoons chopped parsley or cilantro
Salt, to taste
Freshly ground black pepper, to taste

1. Place garlic, ginger, and water in a food processor. Process until smooth.

2. In a large (4-quart) wide saucepan, heat oil over medium flame. Add onion and curry powder and cook, stirring, until onion is tender, about 3 minutes. Toss chicken pieces in flour. Shake off any excess. Increase

heat, add floured chicken pieces and cook until just browned on all sides.

3. Add garlic and ginger purée and stock and gently simmer for 45 minutes, uncovered. Stir in chick-peas, tomatoes, and parsley or cilantro and cook until chicken is fork-tender, about 25 minutes. Season with pepper and salt and serve over rice.

MEXICAN PIE

My family loves this dish. It is hearty, healthy, and full of nutritious ingredients.

Preparation time: 10 minutes
Cooking time: 65 to 70 minutes
Serves 6

   2 cups cornmeal
   1 teaspoon salt
   5 cups water
   1¼ cups shredded reduced-calorie cheddar cheese
   2 tablespoons thinly sliced chives
   ¼ cup finely diced red bell peppers
   Freshly ground black pepper, to taste
   2 tablespoons olive or vegetable oil
   1 cup chopped onion
   1½ cups diced carrot
   2 cloves garlic, minced
   1½ pounds ground beef or turkey
   2½ tablespoons chili powder
   2 teaspoons ground cumin
   1 14-ounce can plum tomatoes, with juice
   3 cups cooked kidney beans
   ½ cup frozen peas, defrosted

1. Preheat oven to 350°F.

2. In a medium saucepan, stir together cornmeal, water, and salt. Heat mixture over a medium-low flame, stirring, until very thick, about 20 minutes. Stir 1 cup of

the cheese, red pepper, chives, and black pepper into mixture.

3. Meanwhile, heat oil in a large, nonstick skillet or wide saucepan, over medium flame. Add onion and cook, stirring until tender, 3 minutes. Add carrot and garlic and continue cooking until onion is golden.

4. Add ground beef or turkey, chili powder, and cumin. Cook, stirring and breaking up meat until browned. Add tomatoes and beans, bring mixture to a boil, reduce heat and simmer for 10 minutes, stirring occasionally. Stir in peas and heat through.

5. Line bottom and sides of a 2-quart casserole with $1/2$ of the cornmeal mixture. Fill casserole with meat and bean mixture. Dot top of casserole with remaining cornmeal mixture and sprinkle with remaining cheese. Bake until casserole is bubbly, about 30 minutes.

LENTIL MEAT LOAF

Here is a healthful alternative to an American classic. By adding lentils to this meat loaf it becomes much higher in fiber and lower in fat, without sacrificing any flavor. An added bonus, this version will fit even the tightest budget!

Preparation time: 10 minutes
Cooking time: 50 minutes
Serves 4 to 5

   1 tablespoon olive oil
   1 1/2 cups chopped onion
   1 cup grated carrot
   2 cloves garlic, minced
   1 1/2 cups water
   1 teaspoon dried thyme
   1 teaspoon ground cumin
   1 teaspoon dried rosemary
   1 teaspoon salt
   1/4 teaspoon nutmeg
   3/4 pound ground beef
   1 egg, lightly beaten
   1/4 cup chopped parsley
   1 tablespoon tiny capers
   3 cups cooked lentils
   1 1/2 cups cooked rice
   2 tablespoons mustard

1. Preheat oven to 350°F.

2. Heat oil in a large nonstick skillet over medium flame. Add onion, carrot, and garlic. Cook, stirring until onion is golden. Stir in water, thyme, cumin, rosemary, salt, and nutmeg.

3. In a large bowl combine beef, egg, parsley, and capers, mixing with hands. Add lentils, rice, and vegetable mixture and mix gently until well combined.

4. Press mixture into a loaf pan and spread surface with mustard. Cover with aluminum foil and bake for 30 minutes. Remove foil and bake another 15 minutes. Allow the meat loaf to rest for 15 minutes before cutting.

YELLOW SPLIT PEA FRITTERS WITH ROASTED RED PEPPER SAUCE

This is an unusual, delicious use for split peas. The accompanying red pepper sauce will soon become a favorite.

Preparation time: 5 minutes, plus 1 hour refrigeration
*Cooking time: 25 to 30 minutes, for fritters; 50 minutes,
  for sauce*
Serves 4 to 5

    1 cup yellow split peas, cooked tender
    ¹/₄ cup bread crumbs
    1 egg
    2 tablespoons low-fat milk
    2 teaspoons olive oil
    1 cup chopped onion
    ¹/₂ cup chopped red pepper
    ¹/₂ cup chopped green pepper
    3 cloves garlic, minced
    1 cup cooked rice
    Salt, to taste
    Freshly ground black pepper, to taste

Sauce:

    3 red bell peppers, seeded and cut in strips
    6 cloves garlic, peeled and split in half
    2 teaspoons olive oil
    1 tablespoon white vinegar
    Water

1. In a food processor, combine $1/2$ cups of the cooked peas, bread crumbs, egg, and milk. Process until smooth, stir in remaining split peas, remove from processor, and refrigerate mixture for 1 hour.

2. Meanwhile, prepare the sauce: Preheat oven to 350°F. Place red peppers and oil in a baking dish. Roast for 30 minutes. Add garlic and continue cooking until peppers are soft and garlic is golden, about 30 minutes. Cool slightly and transfer to food processor. Process with vinegar until smooth. Add water through feed tube, 1 teaspoon at a time, as necessary, to desired consistency.

3. Increase oven temperature to 400°F. Heat oil in a large nonstick skillet, over medium flame. Add onion and cook, stirring, until translucent. Add peppers and garlic and cook until peppers are soft, about 5 minutes. Stir in rice and continue cooking for 1 minute. Season with salt and pepper.

4. Stir rice mixture into the cooled pea purée. Combine well.

5. Using a $1/4$-cup measure, form patties on a lightly oiled nonstick baking sheet. Bake for 10 minutes, turn, and bake 10 minutes on the other side. Serve with red pepper sauce.

BLACK-EYED PEA FRITTATA

This is an intriguing, slightly spicy yet delicate-tasting dish. The fat-free egg substitutes available now are amazing replacements for the cholesterol-laden egg, and are perfect for frittatas.

Preparation time: 5 minutes
Cooking time: 10 to 15 minutes
Serves 4

1 tablespoon olive oil
2 cups tomato, peeled, diced, and seeded
2 tablespoons chopped jalapeño peppers, seeded
$2^{1}/_{2}$ cups cooked black-eyed peas
$^{1}/_{4}$ cup chopped fresh cilantro
$^{1}/_{4}$ teaspoon freshly ground black pepper
$^{1}/_{4}$ teaspoon salt, or to taste
$1^{1}/_{4}$ cups fat-free egg substitute

1. Preheat broiler. Heat oil in a 10-inch nonstick skillet over medium-low flame. Add tomatoes and jalapeños and cook, stirring, until peppers are tender, about 2 minutes.

2. Stir in peas, cilantro, salt, and pepper. Add egg substitute and stir until it begins to set. Continue cooking until almost all of the egg is set, lifting the sides of the frittata to allow the raw egg to run underneath.

3. Place skillet under broiler to finish cooking, 4 to 5 minutes. Keep handle of skillet out of oven to avoid melting it or burning yourself. Slide frittata out onto a plate, cut in wedges and serve.

LIGHT-STYLE BAKED BEANS WITH HAM

This is a lovely version of the classic baked beans. The flavor of pork fat that permeates the classic dish is replaced with the slightly smoky flavor of chopped lean ham.

Preparation time: 5 minutes
Cooking time: 2¹/₂ hours
Serves 4 to 5

1 tablespoon vegetable oil
1 cup chopped onion
1 cup chopped carrot
2 cloves garlic, minced
2 cups canned crushed tomatoes
3 cups cooked navy beans
1 cup water
¹/₃ pound cooked lean ham, diced
¹/₄ cup molasses or honey
1 tablespoon cider vinegar
1 teaspoon mustard powder
¹/₄ teaspoon ground cloves

1. Preheat oven to 325°F.

2. Heat oil in a large nonstick skillet or saucepan over medium-low flame. Add onion, carrot, and garlic and cook, stirring occasionally, until onions are tender. Stir in tomatoes, cover, and cook for 5 minutes.

3. Stir beans, water, ham, molasses or honey, vinegar, mustard powder, and cloves into mixture until well combined.

4. Transfer mixture to a baking dish, and bake, covered with foil for 1 hour. Remove foil and continue cooking for $1^1/_2$ hours.

PROVENÇAL LAMB AND TURKEY-SAUSAGE CASSOULET

Here is a simple, light, yet traditionally flavored cassoulet. It makes a perfect home-cooked meal with a distinct French accent.

Preparation time: 15 minutes
Cooking time: 2¹/₂ hours
Serves 7 to 8

1 pound Great Northern beans, soaked
1 onion studded with 4 cloves
¹/₂ teaspoon freshly ground black pepper
2 pounds lamb, cut in ¹/₂-inch cubes
2 tablespoons flour, seasoned with salt and pepper
2 tablespoons olive oil
1 cup chopped onion
¹/₂ cup chopped carrot
¹/₂ cup chopped celery
3 cloves garlic, minced
16 ounces canned plum tomatoes, including liquid
3 cups veal or chicken stock, reduced-sodium chicken broth or water
1¹/₂ teaspoons fresh thyme leaves or ¹/₂ teaspoon dried thyme
1 bay leaf
¹/₂ pound turkey sausage, sliced into ¹/₂-inch rounds

1. In a large saucepan, place beans, clove-studded onion, and pepper in enough water to cover beans, and sim-

mer until tender, about 1 hour. Drain beans and discard onion.

2. Preheat oven to 375°F. Toss the lamb with flour until well coated. Shake off any excess. Heat oil in a large (4-quart) Dutch oven, and brown floured lamb on all sides over medium heat. Remove with a slotted spoon and set aside.

3. Add onion, carrot, celery, and garlic to pan. Cook, stirring frequently until golden. Return lamb to pan and add tomatoes, stock, thyme, and bay leaf. Bring mixture to a boil and remove promptly from heat. Add beans, sausage, and salt and pepper to taste.

4. Place pot in oven, cover and bake for 30 minutes. Uncover and continue cooking until lamb is tender, about 1 hour.

BLACK-EYED PEA, CHICKEN, AND CARROT STEW

This delicate-tasting stew is best served over brown rice or beside a mound of steaming mashed potatoes.

Preparation time: 5 minutes
Cooking time: 10 minutes
Serves 4

2 tablespoons olive oil
$^{1}/_{2}$ cup chopped shallots
1 pound boneless chicken breast, cut in $^{1}/_{4}$-inch by
    $1^{1}/_{2}$-inch strips
$^{1}/_{2}$ cup flour, seasoned with salt and freshly ground
    black pepper
2 teaspoons dried rosemary leaves
1 teaspoon dried tarragon
$1^{1}/_{2}$ cups sliced carrots
3 cups chicken stock or reduced-sodium chicken
    broth
3 cups cooked black-eyed peas
$^{1}/_{4}$ cup water
2 teaspoons cornstarch
2 teaspoons lemon juice
Salt, to taste
Freshly ground black pepper, to taste

1. Heat oil in a large nonstick skillet over medium flame. Add shallots and cook, stirring until tender. Meanwhile, dredge chicken in flour and shake off excess.

2. Add chicken and herbs to oil, and cook, stirring until chicken is golden. Remove chicken from pan and set aside.

3. Add carrots to skillet and cook for 1 minute. Stir in stock and peas. Stir together water, cornstarch, and lemon juice and add it to the stock. Bring mixture to a boil, stirring constantly. Cook until thickened, about 5 minutes.

4. Return chicken to pan to heat through, and season with salt and pepper.

MOROCCAN-STYLE CHICK-PEA AND VEGETABLE COUSCOUS CASSEROLE

The classic flavors of Morocco are baked together in this lovely casserole. Your family will love this vegetarian treat.

Preparation time: 10 minutes
Cooking time: 65 minutes
Serves 5 to 6

1 tablespoon vegetable oil
1 cup chopped onion
$^1/_2$ cup diced celery
3 cloves garlic, minced
1 28-ounce can plum tomatoes, chopped, including
    liquid
2 cups peeled and diced carrots
$1^1/_2$ teaspoons ground cumin
$^1/_2$ teaspoon freshly ground black pepper
1-inch piece cinnamon stick
1 bay leaf
1 cup water
$^1/_4$ cup chopped parsley
4 cups cooked chick-peas
3 cups cooked couscous

1. Preheat oven to 350°F.

2. Heat oil in a large (4-quart) saucepan over medium flame. Add onions and celery and cook until translucent. Add carrot, garlic, cumin, pepper, cinnamon stick, and bay leaf and continue cooking for 1 minute, stirring.

3. Stir in tomatoes, water, and parsley. Simmer partially covered until carrot is tender, about 35 minutes. Remove cinnamon stick and bay leaf.

4. Stir chick-peas and couscous into mixture. Transfer to a 3-quart baking dish and bake for 30 minutes.

SOUTH AMERICAN MULTI-BEAN CHOWDER

This chowder is based on a soup prepared by the late great chef Felipe Rojas-Lombardi. It is simple and delicious as is, but it is also a lovely base for an even more substantial meal. Feel free to add fish or meat as you desire.

Preparation time: 15 minutes
Cooking time: 1¹/₂ to 2 hours
Serves 6

2 tablespoons olive oil
¹/₂ pound fennel, trimmed and chopped (about 2 cups)
1¹/₂ pounds leek, trimmed, rinsed, and chopped (about 2 cups)
2 stalks celery, chopped (¹/₂ cup)
1 tablespoon grated ginger
2 cloves garlic, minced
³/₄ pound Great Northern beans, soaked
6 cups water
¹/₂ bay leaf
1 dried chili pepper, seeded
1¹/₂ cups diced tomatoes
1¹/₂ cups cooked black-eyed peas
1¹/₂ cups cooked pinto beans
2 cups cooked diced potatoes
¹/₄ cup chopped parsley or cilantro
Salt, to taste
White pepper, to taste

1. Heat oil in a large wide saucepan over medium flame. Add fennel, leeks, and celery. Cook, stirring constantly, until leeks are wilted. Stir in ginger and garlic and continue cooking for 1 minute.

2. Stir in Great Northern beans, water, bay leaf, and chili pepper. Bring mixture to a boil, reduce heat and simmer $1/2$ hour. Remove bay leaf and chili pepper and cool slightly.

3. In batches, transfer mixture to a food processor and process until smooth. Return to saucepan and add black-eyed peas and pinto beans, tomatoes, potatoes, parsley, and salt and pepper. Heat through and serve with lemon wedges.

MAIN DISH SALADS

CHICKEN, CANNELINI BEAN, AND BROCCOLI SALAD WITH CREAMY BASIL DRESSING

This salad is a definite crowd pleaser and is perfect with leftover roast chicken.

Preparation time: 5 minutes
Cooking time: None
Serves 4

2 cups cooked cannelini beans
2 cups cooked chicken, diced
2 cups bite-size broccoli florets, steamed to crisp-tender
2 cups packed fresh basil leaves
$^1/_2$ cup packed flat-leaf parsley
$^1/_4$ cup low-fat or nonfat ricotta cheese
3 cloves garlic, cut up
2 tablespoons pignoli nuts or chopped walnuts
2 tablespoons grated Parmesan cheese
$^1/_2$ teaspoon freshly ground black pepper
$1^1/_2$ tablespoons olive oil
2 tablespoons water
$^1/_4$ teaspoon salt, or to taste

1. Combine beans, chicken, and broccoli in a large bowl. Set aside.

(*Continued on next page*)

2. Place basil, parsley, ricotta, garlic, nuts, cheese, pepper, oil, water, and salt in a food processor and pulse until mixture becomes a smooth paste.

3. Toss basil dressing with beans, chicken, and broccoli until well coated.

Shrimp and Pasta Salad with Cilantro Bean Dressing

This salad is very satisfying while remaining light and very low in fat. Beans are puréed to create a thick dressing that replaces the mayonnaise used in many salads.

Preparation time: 15 minutes
Cooking time: None
Serves 4

> 1 pound large shrimp, cooked, peeled, and
>   deveined
> $1/2$ pound fusilli, radiatore or other pasta shape,
>   cooked
> $1^1/2$ cups diced celery
> 2 cups cooked white beans, any variety
> $1/3$ cup packed cilantro leaves
> 2 tablespoons lime juice
> 1 clove garlic, minced
> 4 or 5 tablespoons water, as necessary
> 1 tablespoon extra-virgin olive oil
> Salt, to taste

1. Combine shrimp, pasta, and celery in a bowl, and set aside.

2. To prepare dressing: Place beans, cilantro, lime juice, and garlic in a food processor. Process until mixture becomes a smooth paste, adding water, one tablespoon at a time, as necessary.   *(Continued on next page)*

3. While the processor is running, slowly add oil, in a thin stream, through the feed tube. Add salt to taste.

4. Toss with shrimp, celery, and pasta and serve on a bed of shredded lettuce.

BLACK BEAN, AVOCADO, AND YELLOW RICE SALAD

This salad was inspired by my regular meal at a local Cuban restaurant: black beans, yellow rice, avocado salad, and a few fiery shots of hot sauce. The combination of beans and rice create a complete protein and thus a healthy meal.

Preparation time: 10 minutes
Cooking time: 20 minutes
Serves 4

2 cups water
1 cup uncooked rice
$^1/_2$ teaspoon powdered turmeric
1 teaspoon vegetable oil
1 teaspoon salt
$2^1/_2$ cups cooked black beans
1 cup diced tomato
$^1/_2$ cup diced roasted red peppers
$^1/_4$ cup chopped sweet white onion
2 tablespoons lemon juice
2 tablespoons olive oil
1 tablespoon white vinegar
Tabasco or other hot sauce, to taste
1 avocado, diced

(Continued on next page)

1. In a medium saucepan, heat water to boiling. Add rice, turmeric, oil, and salt. Cover, lower heat and cook until rice is tender, about 20 minutes. Cool slightly.

2. Combine beans, tomato, red peppers, onion, lemon juice, olive oil, vinegar, and Tabasco. Gently toss with rice and avocado.

Kidney Bean, Chicken, and Mango Salad

This salad makes a healthy and delicious summer meal. Serve it on a bed of shredded lettuce for a beautiful presentation and a crispy crunch!

Preparation time: 8 minutes
Cooking time: None
Serves 6

2 cups cooked chicken, shredded
3 cups cooked kidney beans
1 large ripe mango, cut in chunks
1 medium tomato, peeled, seeded, and diced
³/₄ cup diced cucumber
¹/₄ cup thinly sliced scallion
2 tablespoons chopped walnuts
¹/₃ cup orange juice
2 tablespoons olive oil
1 teaspoon white vinegar
1¹/₂ teaspoons grated ginger
¹/₂ teaspoon salt, or to taste
¹/₂ teaspoon freshly ground black pepper

1. Combine chicken, beans, mango, tomato, cucumber, scallion, and walnuts in a nonmetal bowl.

2. In a separate bowl, combine orange juice, olive oil, vinegar, ginger, pepper, and salt. Toss with mango and bean mixture. Serve alone or on a bed of shredded romaine lettuce.

CLASSIC ITALIAN WHITE BEAN AND TUNA SALAD

The Italians soak their onions in water before adding them to salads. This cuts the sharpness of the onions and brings out their sweetness.

Preparation time: 5 minutes, plus ¹/₂ hour to soak onion
Cooking time: None
Serves 4

¹/₂ clove garlic, unpeeled
3 cups cooked cannelini beans
1 cup thinly sliced red onion, soaked in cold water
    for ¹/₂ hour
1 6¹/₂-ounce can water-packed tuna, flaked
2 tablespoons finely shredded fresh basil leaves
5 teaspoons extra-virgin olive oil
1 tablespoon red wine vinegar
¹/₄ teaspoon freshly ground black pepper, or to taste
Salt, to taste
Radicchio or romaine lettuce leaves

1. Rub a medium-size bowl with the garlic clove. Discard garlic. In the bowl, toss together beans, onion, tuna, basil, oil, vinegar, pepper, and salt.

2. Serve on radicchio or lettuce leaves.

JAPANESE-FLAVOR ADZUKI BEAN SALAD WITH PORK

The flavors of the Far East come alive in this unusual combination of ingredients. Adzuki beans are available at most health food or Asian specialty stores.

Preparation time: 10 minutes
Cooking time: 5 minutes
Serves 4

  $^1/_2$ pound pork loin, diced in $^1/_4$-inch pieces
  2 teaspoons reduced-sodium soy sauce
  2 teaspoons vegetable oil
  2 cups adzuki beans
  1 cup cooked rice
  1 cup chopped radish
  1 cup chopped cucumber
  1 cup chopped mushrooms
  $^1/_4$ cup thinly sliced scallions
Dressing:
  4 strips of lemon zest, cut in $^1/_2$-inch by 2-inch slivers
  2 tablespoons reduced-sodium soy sauce
  2 tablespoons rice wine vinegar
  2 teaspoons finely chopped ginger
  2 teaspoons honey
  $^1/_2$ teaspoon sesame oil

1. Combine pork and 2 teaspoons soy sauce. Heat oil in a large nonstick skillet over medium flame. Add pork and cook until just cooked through.

(*Continued on next page*)

2. In a large bowl, combine pork, beans, rice, radish, cucumber, mushrooms, and scallions, and set aside.

3. In a separate bowl, whisk together lemon zest, soy sauce, vinegar, ginger, honey, and sesame oil. Toss with bean mixture and serve.

PASTAS

RED PEPPER AND TOMATO BEAN SAUCE

This is a wonderful rich tomato and red pepper sauce. It is as thick and hearty as a meat sauce, and rich in low fat vegetable protein. Serve it over a large-shape pasta such as rigatoni.

Preparation time: 10 minutes
Cooking time: 35 minutes
Serves 4 to 5

  2 teaspoons olive oil
  1 cup chopped onion
  4 cloves garlic, minced
  1 1/2 cups chopped red bell pepper
  2 cups canned plum tomatoes
  2 cups cooked pinto beans
  2 cups beef stock, reduced-sodium beef broth, or
    water
  1/2 teaspoon dried thyme
  1/2 teaspoon crushed red pepper
  1/4 teaspoon marjoram
  1 bay leaf
  1 tablespoon vinegar
  Salt, to taste
  Freshly ground black pepper, to taste

1. Heat oil in a large (4-quart) heavy-bottom saucepan over medium flame. Add onion and garlic and cook, stirring until onion is tender, about 3 minutes. Add red

bell pepper and continue cooking until the pepper is tender, another 5 minutes.

2. Add tomatoes, beans, stock, thyme, red pepper, marjoram, and bay leaf. Bring mixture to a boil, reduce heat and simmer, stirring occasionally, for 30 minutes. Remove bay leaf and cool slightly.

3. Transfer ⅔ of the mixture to a food processor and process until chunky-smooth. Return purée to pot and add vinegar, salt, and pepper. Bring to a boil and serve over rigatoni.

PASTA WITH WHITE BEANS AND CLAM SAUCE

Once again, the bean triumphs as the ultimate sauce thickener. The sauce is creamy and rich, yet very light and low in fat compared to flour- or cream-thickened sauces of the past.

Preparation time: 5 minutes
Cooking time: 20 minutes
Serves 4 to 6

  1 pound linguini, shells, or other pasta shape
  1 tablespoon olive oil
  4 cloves garlic, minced
  2 8-ounce bottles clam juice
  3 cups cooked small white beans
  $^1/_2$ teaspoon dried thyme leaves
  2 $6^1/_2$-ounce cans minced clams, including juice
  $^1/_4$ cup chopped parsley
  Salt, to taste
  Freshly ground black pepper, to taste

1. Cook pasta according to package directions. Drain.

2. Heat oil in a large nonstick skillet over medium-low flame. Add garlic and cook, stirring, until tender. Stir in clam juice and juice from the minced clams, then beans and thyme. Simmer for 5 minutes. Cool slightly.

(*Continued on next page*)

3. Transfer the mixture to a food processor and process until smooth.

4. Return mixture to skillet. Add clams, parsley, salt, and pepper and heat through. Toss with cooked pasta and serve.

PASTA AND VEGETABLES WITH CHEESY WHITE BEAN SAUCE

Puréed beans make a lovely rich sauce without the fat of the butter that we're used to. Try serving this dish to the children when you want to sneak them some bean protein.

Preparation time: 15 minutes
Cooking time: 10 minutes, plus pasta cooking time
Serves 4

1 pound penne, or other large pasta shape
2 cups cooked white beans
$^3/_4$ cup low-fat milk
2 teaspoons fresh thyme leaves or $^1/_2$ teaspoon dried thyme
1 cup shredded reduced-fat cheddar cheese
2 tablespoons grated Parmesan cheese
$^1/_2$ teaspoon freshly ground black pepper, or to taste
$^1/_4$ teaspoon grated nutmeg
Salt, to taste
2 cups broccoli florets, cut into 1-inch pieces, steamed to crisp-tender
2 cups cauliflower florets, cut into 1-inch pieces, steamed to crisp-tender
$1^1/_2$ cups quartered cherry tomatoes
$^1/_2$ cup cooked peas
2 tablespoons chopped fresh basil leaves

(*Continued on next page*)

1. Cook pasta according to package directions. Drain.

2. Place beans and milk in a food processor, and process until very smooth.

3. Transfer mixture to a saucepan and heat over medium-low, until just simmering. Stir in cheeses, nutmeg, pepper, and salt. Stir until melted.

4. Toss cheese sauce with pasta, broccoli, cauliflower, tomatoes, peas, and basil and serve.

SPINACH AND CHICK-PEA SHELLS

This is a great homestyle pasta dish, perfect for a hearty meal with friends or family.

Preparation time: 5 minutes
Cooking time: 15 minutes
Serves 4 to 5

1 pound pasta shells
³/₄ cup chopped onion
1 tablespoon olive oil
1¹/₂ cup finely diced red bell pepper
2 cups cooked chick-peas
3 tablespoons chopped fresh dill
1 cup water
¹/₂ cup tomato paste (1 small can)
¹/₂ teaspoon freshly ground black pepper, or to taste
Salt, to taste
3¹/₂ cups chopped spinach leaves
2 tablespoons pignoli (pine) nuts

1. Cook pasta shells until tender, drain and set aside.

2. In a large nonstick skillet, cook onion in oil over medium heat a few minutes, until tender. Add red pepper and continue cooking until peppers are tender. Add chick-peas and dill and toss to coat.

(*Continued on next page*)

3. Stir in the water, tomato paste, pepper, and salt. Cover and simmer for 5 minutes.

4. Add spinach to chick-peas and cook until just wilted. Toss pasta shells with sauce and pignoli nuts. Serve promptly.

MEXICAN LASAGNE

Think of the surprise at the first bite of this lasagne when everyone tastes the unconventional fillings. And then think of the smiles, bravos, and requests for it in the future.

Preparation time: 30 minutes
Cooking time: 45 to 55 minutes
Serves 6

   $1/2$ pound lasagne noodles
   2 tablespoons olive oil
   2 medium onions, thinly sliced
   2 red peppers, cored and cut in $1/8$-inch-wide strips
   2 green peppers, cored and cut in $1/8$-inch-wide strips
   2 medium zucchini, sliced $1/8$-inch thick
   2 yellow squash, sliced $1/8$-inch thick
   Salt, to taste
   Freshly ground black pepper, to taste
   1 tablespoon vegetable oil
   3 cups cooked kidney, pinto, or black beans
   3 cloves garlic, minced
   2 teaspoons chili powder
   1 teaspoon ground cumin
   $1/8$ teaspoon cayenne pepper
   $1/2$ cup water
   $2^1/2$ cups homemade or canned tomato sauce
   1 cup shredded reduced-fat cheddar cheese

1. Preheat oven to 300°F.

(Continued on next page)

2. Cook lasagne noodles in plenty of water, until just tender. Drain and place in cold water until needed.

3. Heat 2 tablespoons olive oil in a large nonstick skillet over medium flame. Add onion and cook, stirring until soft. Add peppers, zucchini, and squash and cook until tender, about 20 minutes. Season with salt and pepper to taste.

4. Meanwhile, heat 1 tablespoon vegetable oil in a large nonstick skillet over medium-low flame. Add garlic, chili powder, cumin, and cayenne pepper and cook for 1 minute. Stir in beans, add water, cover, and cook for 3 minutes. Cool slightly.

5. Place cooled bean mixture in a food processor. Process until smooth and spreadable (add a little water, if necessary).

6. In a 9-inch by 13-inch lasagne pan, spread $1/2$ cup tomato sauce, and layer pasta sheets, $1/2$ of the bean mixture, then $1/2$ cup sauce, $1/2$ of the vegetable mixture, and $1/3$ cup cheese; repeat. Spread top with remaining sauce and sprinkle with remaining cheese.

7. Bake until cheese is melted and sauce is bubbly, about 45 minutes. Allow lasagne to sit for 10 minutes before cutting.

SALADS

SOUTHWESTERN BLACK BEAN SALAD

This is a flavorful and colorful salad. But feel free to break from the Southwest theme by eating it, as I do, stuffed in a pita with shredded romaine lettuce.

Preparation time: 5 minutes
Cooking time: None
Serves 4

1 tablespoon ground cumin
2 tablespoons lime juice
1 tablespoon extra-virgin olive or vegetable oil
1 teaspoon white vinegar
1/4 teaspoon salt
1 1/2 cups cooked black beans
1/2 cup finely diced carrot
1/2 cup cooked corn kernels
3 tablespoons chopped cilantro
2 tablespoons chopped red onion

1. Heat cumin in a small skillet over a low flame just until fragrant, about 1 minute.

2. Whisk together cumin, lime juice, oil, and salt.

3. Combine beans, carrot, corn, cilantro, and onion. Toss with dressing.

LEMONY WHITE BEAN SALAD

I could eat this salad every day! Make a large batch and reserve leftovers; each day that it stays in the refrigerator, it gets better tasting. You can use canned beans, but I prefer this method because hot beans absorb the flavors much better.

Preparation time: 5 minutes, plus cooling and marination time.
Cooking time: About 2 hours
Serves 5 to 6

    2 cups small white beans, soaked
    1 clove garlic
    1 teaspoon salt
    1 cup thinly sliced scallions
    ¼ cup lemon juice
    3 tablespoons extra-virgin olive oil
    1 tablespoon white vinegar
    ¼ cup chopped fresh parsley
    1 tablespoon chopped dill
    1 teaspoon chopped fresh mint

1. In a medium saucepan, place beans in enough water to cover and cook until tender but not broken, about 2 hours. Drain well and transfer to a bowl.

2. Chop garlic with salt and add it to hot beans along with scallions, lemon juice, oil, and vinegar. Toss well and set aside until cool.

3. Add chopped herbs and refrigerate salad for at least 1 hour before serving.

HERBED FRENCH LENTIL SALAD

This is a classic, delicious salad—flecked with herbs. Be sure not to overcook the lentils—they should remain whole!

Preparation time: 5 minutes, plus cooling time
Cooking time: 20 to 30 minutes
Serves 4

   1 cup lentils
   1 bay leaf
   $^1/_2$ cup finely diced red bell pepper
   $^1/_2$ cup finely diced green bell pepper
   $^1/_2$ cup chopped sweet white onion
   2 tablespoons chopped parsley
   2 tablespoons extra-virgin olive oil
   1 tablespoon chopped fresh sage
   1 tablespoon white wine vinegar
   Salt, to taste
   Freshly ground pepper, to taste

1. In a medium saucepan, place lentils with bay leaf in plenty of boiling water, and cook until just tender, 20 to 30 minutes. Drain well and remove bay leaf.

2. Toss hot lentils with peppers, onions, parsley, oil, sage, vinegar, salt, and pepper. Cool to room temperature and serve.

MARINATED THREE-BEAN SALAD

Three beautiful colors and crisp flavors make this salad a simple treat. Marinate it overnight for a really wonderful taste.

Preparation time: 5 minutes
Cooking time: 3 minutes
Serves 4

$1/2$ pound fresh green beans, trimmed and cut into
   1-inch lengths
$1/4$ cup red wine vinegar
4 teaspoons extra-virgin olive oil
$1/4$ cup shredded fresh basil leaves
$1/4$ teaspoon freshly ground black pepper
1 teaspoon sugar
$1^1/2$ cups red bell pepper cut into 1-inch by $1/4$-inch
   strips
1 cup cooked red kidney beans
1 cup cooked chick-peas

1. Bring a large pot of water to the boil. Cook green beans just until crisp-tender, about 3 minutes. Drain.

2. Whisk together vinegar, oil, basil, pepper, and sugar.

3. Place hot green beans and red pepper strips in a shallow dish. Add cooked beans, pour marinade over, and gently toss. Cover and marinate for at least one hour. Serve chilled.

PINTO BEAN SALAD WITH HAM

This is a lovely light bean salad which packs a very robust flavor. Try serving it hot as a side dish by heating it quickly in a nonstick skillet.

Preparation time: 8 minutes
Cooking time: None
Serves 4

> 3 cups pinto beans
> 1¹/₂ cups diced celery
> ¹/₂ cup diced cooked ham
> 2 tablespoons crumbled blue cheese (optional)
> 3 tablespoons chopped fresh dill
> 3 tablespoons chopped fresh parsley
> 2 tablespoons red wine vinegar
> 1 tablespoon extra-virgin olive oil
> 2 cloves garlic, minced
> 1 teaspoon chopped fresh sage or ¹/₂ teaspoon dried
>   sage (if using dry, chop with parsley)
> ¹/₄ teaspoon freshly ground black pepper

1. In a bowl combine beans, celery, ham, and cheese if desired. Set aside.

2. In a separate bowl, whisk together dill, parsley, vinegar, oil, garlic, sage, and pepper. Toss with bean mixture and serve.

ROMAN KIDNEY BEAN SALAD

This is a version of an Italian poor-man's salad. Originally made with day-old bread, this salad has the robust flavors of a feast.

Preparation time: 10 minutes, plus ¹/₂ hour marination time
Cooking time: None
Serves 4

4 anchovy filets
1 tablespoon capers, drained
1 clove garlic, minced
Pinch salt
1 tablespoon olive oil
2 teaspoons red wine vinegar
1 teaspoon lemon juice
2 cups cooked kidney beans
1 cup tomato diced
1 cup diced celery
¹/₃ cup chopped red onion

1. Chop anchovies and capers with garlic and salt until mixture is almost smooth. Transfer paste to a small bowl and whisk it together with oil, vinegar, and lemon juice.

2. Combine kidney beans, tomato, celery, and onion in a large nonmetal bowl. Toss with anchovy mixture and refrigerate for 30 minutes.

BARLEY BEAN SALAD

Here is a lovely, refreshing salad which is hearty enough for a meal. Served on a bed of mixed greens, it makes a colorful, festive dish.

Preparation time: 5 minutes
Cooking time: None
Serves 6

3 cups cooked black beans
2 cups cooked barley
1¹/₂ cups cooked yellow corn
1 cup diced red bell pepper
4 scallions, thinly sliced
3 tablespoons extra-virgin olive oil
3 tablespoons balsamic or red wine vinegar
2 tablespoons lime juice
Salt, to taste
Freshly ground black pepper, to taste

1. In a large nonmetal bowl, combine black beans, barley, corn, red pepper, and scallion.

2. In a separate bowl, whisk together oil, vinegar, lime juice, salt, and pepper. Toss with bean mixture.

WHITE BEAN AND WATERCRESS SALAD WITH TOMATO DRESSING

By vigorously stirring the tomatoes with the other dressing ingredients they give up their juice. This becomes the base of the dressing. The other ingredients round out the Italian flavor of the dish.

Preparation time: 5 minutes
Cooking time: None
Serves 4

> 2 cups cooked small white beans
> 1 cup torn watercress or arugula leaves
> 2 cups slivered cherry tomatoes
> 6 olives, pitted and slivered
> 2 tablespoons shredded basil leaves
> 1 tablespoon extra-virgin olive oil
> 2 teaspoons red wine vinegar
> 1 clove garlic, minced
> ¹/₄ teaspoon freshly ground black pepper
> 1 tablespoon grated Parmesan cheese

1. In a large bowl, mix together the beans and watercress or arugula leaves. Set aside.

2. In a separate bowl, combine tomatoes, olives, basil, olive oil, vinegar, garlic, and pepper. Stir vigorously until well combined. Toss with beans, watercress, and Parmesan.

SUCCOTASH VINAIGRETTE

Lima beans grow up! This is nothing like the succotash you remember. It has a lovely sophisticated flavor that you and your family will love.

Preparation time: 5 minutes
Cooking time: 5 to 6 minutes
Serves 4

1 cup frozen corn kernels
1 teaspoon dijon mustard
1¹/₂ tablespoons balsamic or good red wine vinegar
1 tablespoon extra-virgin olive oil
2 cups cooked dried lima beans
¹/₄ cup finely diced red onion
¹/₄ cup diced red bell pepper
Salt, to taste
Freshly ground black pepper, to taste

1. Cook corn until tender, about 5 or 6 minutes.

2. Meanwhile, whisk together the mustard and vinegar. Slowly add oil to mixture while whisking. Toss with lima beans, corn, onion, and red pepper. Sprinkle with salt and pepper. Cool before serving.

BLACK-EYED PEA SALAD WITH LEMON AND MINT

This is such a simple salad, but it is so fresh and delicious. Serve it in the summer with chicken fresh off the grill, or at an all-salad luncheon.

Preparation time: 5 minutes
Cooking time: None
Serves 4

    3 cups cooked black-eyed peas
    2 cups diced cucumber
    1 cup diced seeded tomato
    6 tablespoons chopped fresh mint
    1/4 cup thinly sliced scallions
    2 tablespoons lemon juice
    4 teaspoons extra-virgin olive oil
    Salt, to taste

1. In a large nonmetal bowl, combine peas, cucumber, tomato, mint, and scallions.

2. Whisk together oil, lemon juice, and salt. Toss with pea mixture. Serve cool.

LENTIL AND ORANGE SALAD

This combination of lentils and orange is a brilliant contrast. The slightly nutty flavor of the lentils complement the sweet and sour of the orange—an exotic treat!

Preparation time: 5 minutes
Cooking time: None
Serves 4 to 5

    4 cups cooked lentils
    2 large oranges, sectioned, peel and pith removed
    $1/2$ cup chopped red onion
    $1/4$ cup thinly shredded basil leaves
    2 tablespoons apple cider vinegar
    4 teaspoons extra-virgin olive oil
    $1/4$ teaspoon salt, or to taste

1. In a large nonmetal bowl, combine lentils, orange, onion, and basil.

2. Whisk together vinegar, oil, and salt. Toss with lentil and orange mixture. Serve at room temperature.

FRUITED WILD RICE AND BEAN SALAD

Everyone loves this healthy salad—crunchy and sweet—it's a must for the buffet table.

Preparation time: 10 minutes, plus cooling time
Cooking time: 45 minutes
Serves 6

1 cup wild rice
5 cups chicken stock or reduced-sodium chicken broth
3 cups cooked small red beans
3/4 cup golden raisins
1/2 cup broken pecans
1/3 cup thinly sliced scallions
1/4 cup chopped fresh mint
1 tablespoon grated orange zest
2 cans mandarin orange sections, including liquid
2 tablespoons extra-virgin olive oil
Salt, to taste
Freshly ground black pepper, to taste
1 cup grapes, halved

1. In a large saucepan, bring stock to a boil. Stir in wild rice, reduce heat and simmer, uncovered, until tender, about 45 minutes. Drain well and transfer to a large bowl.

(Continued on next page)

2. Add beans, raisins, nuts, scallion, mint, orange zest, mandarin oranges, oil, pepper, and salt. Toss well. Cover and let salad cool to room temperature.

3. Add grapes and serve at room temperature or refrigerate and serve cool.

CRUNCHY CURRIED YELLOW SPLIT PEA, BROWN RICE, AND APPLE SALAD

Split peas can be a different and delicious addition to your salad repertoire. Cook them until they are just tender. If cooked too long they will get mushy.

Preparation time: 10 minutes
Cooking time: 1 minute
Serves 5 to 6

2 cups yellow split peas, cooked until just tender
1¹/₂ cups cooked brown rice
1 cup chopped red delicious apple
1 cup chopped celery
¹/₂ cup chopped onion
¹/₂ cup chopped carrot
¹/₃ cup diced red bell pepper
¹/₄ cup golden raisins
1¹/₂ teaspoons curry powder
Pinch cinnamon
¹/₃ cup low-fat yogurt
3 tablespoons reduced-fat mayonnaise
2 teaspoons cider vinegar

1. In a large bowl, combine peas, rice, apple, celery, onion, carrots, pepper, and raisins and set aside.

2. In a small skillet, heat curry powder and cinnamon over very low flame until just fragrant, about 1 minute. Combine yogurt, mayonnaise, and vinegar. Stir in curry mixture and toss with yellow pea and rice mixture. Serve cool.

Chick-Pea and Macaroni Salad

This is a healthy twist on the classic macaroni salad. The usual mayonnaise is replaced by light mayonnaise and low-fat yogurt and the nutrition is boosted with chick-peas.

Preparation time: 10 minutes
Cooking time: None
Serves 6

   3 cups cooked chick-peas
   3 cups cooked macaroni
   ¹/₂ cup chopped celery
   ¹/₄ cup low-fat yogurt
   ¹/₄ cup chopped red pepper
   ¹/₄ cup chopped green pepper
   3 tablespoons chopped onion
   2 tablespoons light mayonnaise
   1 tablespoon red wine vinegar
   Freshly ground black pepper, to taste

1. In a large bowl, combine chick-peas, macaroni, celery, yogurt, peppers, onion, mayonnaise, vinegar, and pepper. Toss well and serve.

SIDE DISHES

REFRIED BEANS

Refried beans is a traditional Mexican dish; but it is also delicious with other flavors. Here I have given a choice between the traditional Mexican and Indian flavorings.

Preparation time: 2 minutes
Cooking time: 12 to 15 minutes
Serves 5 to 6

1½ tablespoons vegetable oil
2 cups chopped onion
3 cloves garlic, minced
2 teaspoons curry *or* chili powder
4 cups cooked pinto beans
Water
2 tablespoons thinly sliced chives
Salt, to taste

1. Heat oil in a large nonstick skillet over medium-low flame. Add onion, garlic, and curry or chili powder. Cook, stirring until onion is tender.

2. Add 1 tablespoon water and beans, ¼ cup at a time, mashing them into onion. Mixture should be fairly dry, but if it becomes too dry, mix in more water, 1 tablespoon at a time, until fully mashed.

3. Add chives and salt and mix thoroughly. Serve promptly.

LIGHT-STYLE CUBAN BLACK BEANS

Serve this classic dish with white, yellow, or brown rice. A large plate of beans and rice with a salad makes a hearty, healthful, and inexpensive meal. Keep a bottle of hot sauce on hand, for authenticity and a bit of zing.

Preparation time: 5 minutes
Cooking time: 1¹/₂ hours
Serves 4

   ¹/₂ pound soaked black beans
   3 cups water
   1¹/₂ cups chopped onion
   1 cup chopped green pepper
   ¹/₄ cup packed fresh cilantro leaves
   ¹/₂ teaspoon oregano
   1 bay leaf
   2 tablespoons olive oil
   1 clove garlic, minced
   ¹/₂ cup diced red pepper
   2 tablespoons vinegar
   Pinch sugar
   Salt, to taste

1. In a 3-quart saucepan, combine beans, water, ³/₄ cup of onion, ¹/₂ cup of green pepper, cilantro, oregano, and bay leaf. Bring to a boil, reduce heat immediately, and simmer until beans are very tender, about 1¹/₂ hours. There should be some liquid left. If you see that too

much liquid is evaporating during cooking, add a little more water.

2. Meanwhile, heat oil in a nonstick skillet over medium flame, add garlic, red peppers, remaining green peppers, and remaining onion. Cook, stirring, until vegetables are tender.

3. Stir vegetables into cooked beans, along with vinegar, sugar, and salt. Mash a few beans against side of pan, to thicken mixture. Heat to boiling and serve over rice.

MASHED SPLIT PEAS AND POTATOES

This is a wonderful, fresh and nutritious alternative to plain mashed potatoes. Use your imagination to experiment with other additions.

Preparation time: 10 minutes
Cooking time: 30 to 35 minutes
Serves 6

   2 tablespoons olive oil
   1 1/2 cups chopped onion
   2 cloves garlic, minced
   3 cups peeled, cubed potatoes
   1 1/2 cups yellow split peas
   2 cups chicken broth or reduced-sodium chicken
       broth
   2 1/2 cups water
   1/2 teaspoon ground cumin
   1 cup diced tomatoes
   2 tablespoons chopped olives
   2 tablespoons lemon juice
   2 teaspoons fresh thyme leaves
   Salt, to taste

1. Heat olive oil in a large saucepan over medium-high flame. Add onions and garlic and cook until tender. Stir in potatoes and continue cooking until onions just begin to turn golden.

2. Stir in peas, broth, water, and cumin. Bring to a boil, lower heat, and simmer, partially covered, until peas are tender, 30 to 35 minutes. Drain.

3. Transfer drained mixture to a large bowl and mash with a potato masher. When mixture is smooth, stir in tomatoes, olives, lemon juice, thyme, and salt.

LENTILS WITH SPINACH AND GINGER

Lentils aren't just for soup anymore! Try this lovely sautéed lentil dish for a tasty change at dinner.

Preparation time: 5 minutes
Cooking time: 15 minutes
Serves 4

2 teaspoons olive oil
1/2 cup chopped onion
2 cloves garlic
1/2 cup finely diced red bell pepper
1/2 cup finely diced carrot
1 tablespoon grated ginger
2 cups cooked lentils
1 10-ounce package frozen chopped spinach,
    defrosted and drained
1 cup water
1 teaspoon reduced-sodium soy sauce

1. Heat oil in a large nonstick skillet over medium flame. Add onion and garlic and cook, stirring, until onion is transluscent. Add red pepper, carrot, and ginger and continue cooking until onion is golden.

2. Stir in lentils, spinach, and water, cover and simmer for 10 minutes. Sprinkle with soy sauce and serve.

LIMA BEANS WITH LEMON AND POPPY SEEDS

The flavors of this lima bean dish are classic and simple. Try serving them at an elegant dinner. They look beautiful on the plate.

Preparation time: 5 minutes
Cooking time: 10 to 12 minutes
Serves 4

1 tablespoon olive oil
1 clove garlic, minced
3 cups cooked dried lima beans
1¹/₂ cups chicken stock, reduced-sodium chicken broth or water
¹/₄ cup, plus 2 tablespoons lemon juice
1 teaspoon grated lemon zest
1 teaspoon cornstarch
¹/₂ cup scallions
2 tablespoons poppy seeds

1. Heat oil in a large nonstick skillet over medium-low flame. Add garlic and cook, stirring, for 1 minute. Add beans, 1 cup stock, ¹/₄ cup lemon juice, and lemon zest. Simmer until flavors are combined, 6 to 7 minutes.

2. Meanwhile, whisk remaining stock and lemon juice with cornstarch. Stir cornstarch mixture into beans. Bring it to a boil and cook, stirring constantly, until sauce has thickened. Toss limas with scallions and poppy seeds and serve promptly.

GREEK-STYLE BRAISED CHICK-PEAS

This is a lovely dish that my Greek-American friend, Rhea, makes for me as her grandmother did, and her mother still does, for her. Served with rice, it can be a simple meal.

Preparation time: 5 minutes
Cooking time: 30 minutes
Serves 6

    1 tablespoon olive oil
    2 cups chopped onion
    3 cloves garlic, minced
    1 14-ounce can plum tomatoes, including liquid
    1 cup water
    4 cups cooked chick-peas
    1/3 cup chopped parsley
    1/4 cup chopped fresh mint
    3 tablespoons lemon juice
    Salt, to taste
    1/2 teaspoon freshly ground black pepper

1. Heat oil in a large saucepan over medium-low flame. Add onion and garlic and cook, stirring, until just tender. Stir in tomatoes and water and continue cooking for 1 minute.

2. Add chick-peas, parsley, and mint. Bring mixture to a boil, reduce heat, and gently simmer for 20 minutes. Add lemon juice, salt, and pepper and cook for 5 minutes.

GARLICKY WHITE BEANS AND ESCAROLE

This dish is for garlic lovers only! But don't be alarmed; the garlic is well mellowed by the beans and a bit of cooking.

Preparation time: 10 minutes
Cooking time: 15 minutes
Serves 6

1 tablespoon olive oil
8 cloves garlic, minced
3 cups cooked Great Northern beans
1 cup diced plum tomato
1 cup water
1 tablespoon white vinegar
4 cups torn escarole leaves
Salt, to taste
Freshly ground black pepper, to taste

1. Heat oil in a large nonstick skillet over medium-low flame. Add garlic and cook, stirring, until tender.

2. Add beans and tomato and stir to coat. Add water and vinegar, cover, and cook for 5 minutes.

3. Stir in escarole, add salt and pepper, cover, and cook, stirring occasionally until escarole is tender but still bright green, 5 to 6 minutes.

CANNELINI MARGHERITA

Cannelini beans are lovely combined with the flavors of a classic Italian pizza topping—tomatoes, basil, and cheese. The children will love this dish because the flavors are familiar to them. Add little bits of pepperoni or sausage to continue the theme.

Preparation time: 3 minutes
Cooking time: 5 minutes
Serves 4

   2 teaspoons olive oil
   1 clove garlic, minced
   1 cup chopped canned plum tomatoes, without liquid
   2 cups cooked cannelini beans, rinse and drain if
      canned
   2 tablespoons chopped fresh basil
   2 tablespoons grated Parmesan

1. Heat oil in a large nonstick saucepan over medium-low flame. Add garlic and cook, stirring, until tender.

2. Stir in tomatoes and beans. Simmer for 3 minutes, stirring occasionally.

3. Sprinkle with basil and Parmesan, stir well and serve.

VEGETABLE BEAN CASSEROLE PARMESAN

This lovely bean casserole has the robust flavor of Parmesan cheese and a beautiful sauce made from natural vegetable juices.

Preparation time: 10 minutes
Cooking time: 55 minutes
Serves 4 to 6

2 red bell peppers, slivered
2 cups diced tomatoes
2 cups onion, slivered
1 cup diagonally sliced celery
4 cloves garlic, slivered
1 teaspoon fresh thyme leaves
$1/2$ teaspoon dried oregano
1 tablespoon olive oil
3 cups cooked kidney beans
2 cups water
3 tablespoons grated Parmesan cheese
Freshly ground black pepper, to taste

1. Preheat oven to 375°F.

2. Toss peppers, tomato, onion, celery, garlic, thyme, and oregano with olive oil. Place in oven and roast for 35 minutes, tossing occasionally.

3. Stir in beans and water and return to oven for 20 minutes. Toss with cheese and pepper.

SMOTHERED BEANS WITH SAUSAGE AND PEPPERS

This slow-cooked bean dish has a rich smoky taste. The sausage has a lot of flavor, but since so little is used, the fat content of the dish is still quite low.

Preparation time: 5 minutes
Cooking time: 45 to 50 minutes
Serves 4 to 5

> 2 ounces sausage meat, removed from casing
> 2 cups pinto beans
> 1 cup diced red bell pepper
> 1 cup diced green bell pepper
> 1 cup chopped onion
> ³/₄ cup chicken stock or reduced-sodium chicken broth
> 3 cloves garlic, minced
> Salt, to taste
> Freshly ground black pepper, to taste

1. Cook sausage in a large nonstick skillet over medium heat, breaking it up as it is stirred. When sausage is cooked, remove from pan, wipe pan clean, and return sausage to pan.

2. Add beans, peppers, onion, stock, and garlic, cover and cook over medium heat for 40 minutes, stirring occasionally. Add salt and pepper, to taste.

ORANGY SWEET POTATO WITH RED AND WHITE KIDNEY BEANS

This is a wonderful homey dish perfect with chicken, turkey or game. Don't worry about overcooking the beans; the acid in the orange juice will keep them from getting too soft.

Preparation time: 5 minutes
Cooking time: 75 to 90 minutes
Serves 4 to 5

> 2 cups cubed (¹/₂-inch) peeled sweet potatoes
> 1 cup cooked red kidney beans
> 1 cup cooked white kidney beans
> 1¹/₂ cups orange juice
> 2 teaspoons olive oil
> ³/₄ teaspoon dried sage
> 1 clove garlic, minced
> ¹/₂ teaspoon salt
> Pinch ground cloves

1. Preheat oven to 375°F. Place potatoes in a 1-quart casserole. Top with beans.

2. Stir together orange juice, olive oil, sage, garlic, salt, and cloves. Pour juice mixture over sweet potato and beans. Place in oven and cook, stirring two or three times, until potatoes are tender, 75 to 90 minutes. Allow dish to cool for 5 minutes before serving.

CANNELINI BEANS AND POTATOES GREMOLATA

Gremolata is the brilliant combination of parsley, lemon zest, garlic, and pepper. Sprinkled over potatoes and beans it makes a lovely dish.

Preparation time: 5 minutes
Cooking time: 20 to 25 minutes
Serves 4

 1 pound small red new potatoes
 2 cups cooked cannelini beans
 2 tablespoons extra-virgin olive oil
 1/3 cup chopped parsley
 3 cloves garlic, minced
 1 tablespoon grated lemon zest
 1 teaspoon salt
 3/4 teaspoon freshly ground black pepper

1. Boil potatoes in plenty of water until tender, 20 to 25 minutes. Drain potatoes well and slice 1/4-inch thick. Heat beans until just warm. Toss warm potatoes and beans with olive oil.

2. To prepare the gremolata: Combine parsley, garlic, lemon zest, salt, and pepper and chop all together until very fine. Sprinkle the gremolata over warm potatoes and beans.

PIGEON PEAS AND TOMATO RICE

This is a very flavorful dish cooked in just enough bacon to give a slightly smoky aroma and little enough oil to keep it light. Serve it as a side dish, but remember, it has all the nutrition to be served as a meal by itself.

Preparation time: 5 minutes
Cooking time: 35 to 40 minutes
Serves 6

   2 strips bacon, chopped
   1 cup chopped onion
   2 cloves garlic, minced
   1 cup rice
   $^1/_2$ pound pigeon peas, cooked (4 to 5 cups)
   1 14-ounce can plum tomatoes, juice reserved
   $1^3/_4$ to 2 cups chicken stock or reduced-sodium
      chicken broth
   $^1/_2$ teaspoon crushed hot red pepper flakes
   $^1/_4$ teaspoon salt
   Pinch allspice
   1 bay leaf

1. Slowly cook bacon in a large wide saucepan until crisp. Pour off excess fat but do not wipe pan. Add onion and garlic to pan and cook over medium heat, stirring, until tender.

2. Stir rice into onion and bacon mixture, just to coat. Add peas, tomatoes, reserved tomato juice plus stock

to make $2^1/_4$ cups, hot pepper flakes, salt, allspice, and bay leaf.

3. Heat mixture to boiling. Cover, reduce heat, and simmer until liquid is absorbed, about 30 minutes. Remove bay leaf. Serve hot.

BROWN RICE AND RED BEAN PILAF

This pilaf has a brilliant sweetness and the intriguing flavors of the Middle East. Don't forget, the combination of rice and beans makes a complete protein and children will enjoy this healthful side dish, even if they don't eat their main course.

Preparation time: 5 minutes
Cooking time: 45 to 50 minutes
Serves 4 to 5

- 1 tablespoon vegetable oil
- 1 cup chopped onion
- 1 tablespoon chopped orange zest
- 1-inch cinnamon stick
- $^1/_2$ teaspoon ground cumin
- 1 cup long grain brown rice
- 2 tablespoons currants
- 2$^1/_2$ cups chicken stock, reduced-sodium chicken broth or water
- $^1/_2$ teaspoon sugar
- $^1/_2$ teaspoon salt
- 2 cups cooked red beans

1. Heat oil in a large (4-quart) wide saucepan over medium flame. Add onions and cook, stirring, until tender. Stir in orange zest, cinnamon stick, and cumin, then rice and currants. Stir to coat.

(Continued on next page)

2. Add stock, sugar, and salt and bring mixture to a boil. Reduce heat, cover, and simmer over a very low flame for 35 minutes.

3. Stir beans into rice and continue cooking until rice is tender, about 10 minutes. If there is liquid in the mixture, uncover pot, increase heat, and stir gently until it has evaporated.

HERBED HOPPIN' JOHN

This is an updated verson of the classic Hoppin' John. Its flavors are bright and fresh and it is very pretty on the plate.

Preparation time: 5 minutes
Cooking time: 5 minutes
Serves 6

4 teaspoons olive oil
1 cup chopped onion
1 cup diced tomato
3 cups cooked black-eyed peas
3 cups cooked rice
3 tablespoons chopped parsley
1 tablespoon chopped basil leaves
1 tablespoon chopped fresh rosemary, thyme leaves
    or a combination
$^1/_2$ teaspoon salt, or to taste
Freshly ground black pepper, to taste

1. Heat oil in a large nonstick skillet over medium flame. Add onion and cook, stirring, until translucent. Add tomato and cook for 1 minute more.

2. Stir in peas, rice, parsley, basil, and rosemary or thyme and continue cooking, tossing gently, for 3 minutes. Season with salt and pepper.

SWEETS

RASPBERRY ALMOND BEAN PIE

Who would believe that puréed beans would make such a fabulous filling for a pie? Creamy and custardy, it's perfectly offset by the slight tartness of the raspberries.

Preparation time: 5 minutes
Cooking time: 60 to 70 minutes
Serves 6

> 1 prepared pie crust, homemade or store-bought
> 2 cups cooked cannelini beans
> 1/4 cup, plus 2 tablespoons sugar
> 1/4 cup low-fat milk
> 1 egg
> 2 teaspoons grated lemon zest
> 1 teaspoon almond or vanilla extract
> 1 12-ounce package frozen raspberries, defrosted slightly
> 2 tablespoons sugar
> 1 tablespoon cornstarch
> 2 tablespoons sliced almonds

1. Preheat oven to 375°F. Prick bottom and sides of crust and bake until it is just beginning to color, 10 to 12 minutes. Reduce oven temperature to 350°F.

2. Meanwhile, combine beans, 1/4 cup of sugar, milk, egg, lemon zest, and almond extract in a food processor and process until smooth. *(Continued on next page)*

3. Toss raspberries with remaining sugar and cornstarch. Spread $^1/_2$ of raspberry mixture on bottom of crust. Pour bean mixture over them and dot top with remaining raspberry mixture. Sprinkle with almonds.

4. Bake for 50 to 60 minutes until filling is firm and lightly golden on top.

MOLASSES BEAN SOUFFLÉ WITH LEMON-GINGER SAUCE

Don't let this recipe intimidate you. It's easy to make and is a perfect ending to a winter meal.

Preparation time: 10 minutes
Cooking time: 35 to 40 minutes
Serves 5 to 6

Soufflé:

- 2 cups cooked pinto beans
- 1 cup low-fat milk
- 1/2 cup molasses
- 2 tablespoons sherry
- 1 tablespoon chopped ginger
- 1 tablespoon vegetable oil
- 1 teaspoon allspice
- 1/2 teaspoon nutmeg
- 1/4 teaspoon ground cloves
- 3 egg whites

Sauce:

- 1/4 cup lemon juice
- 1/4 cup sugar
- 3 tablespoons sherry
- 3 tablespoons currants
- 1 tablespoon grated ginger

1. Preheat oven to 325°F. *(Continued on next page)*

2. In a food processor, combine beans, milk, molasses, sherry, oil, ginger, allspice, nutmeg, and cloves. Process until smooth and transfer mixture to a large bowl.

3. Beat egg whites until stiff and gently fold them into bean mixture. Pour batter into a 1-quart baking dish. Bake until puffed and golden, 35 to 40 minutes.

4. To prepare sauce: Combine lemon juice, sugar, sherry, currants, and ginger in a small saucepan. Heat to boiling over medium flame, stirring constantly. Cook until currants are plump, about 3 minutes.

5. Serve soufflé warm, drizzled with sauce.

ORANGY RICE AND BEAN PUDDING

This pudding is gratefully dedicated to Marie Simmons, author of *Rice: The Amazing Grain*, and rice pudding maker extraordinaire! Served warm or cold it makes a delicious dessert or breakfast treat.

Preparation time: 5 minutes
Cooking time: 45 to 50 minutes
Serves 4 to 6

  2 teaspoons vegetable oil
  1 cup long-grain brown rice
  1 tablespoon chopped orange zest
  1-inch cinnamon stick
  2¹/₂ cups water
  ¹/₄ cup, plus 1 tablespoon sugar
  2 cups cooked adzuki beans
  ³/₄ cup low-fat milk
  ¹/₂ cup diced orange segments, pith removed
  ¹/₂ teaspoon vanilla extract
  Ground cinnamon, to garnish

1. Heat oil in a large saucepan over medium-low flame. Add rice, orange zest, and cinnamon stick. Stir to coat. Stir in water and 1 tablespoon sugar, and bring mixture to a boil. Reduce heat and simmer, covered, for 30 minutes.

2. Add beans to rice, stir once, and continue cooking until rice is tender. If there is still liquid in the pan, in-

crease heat and stir until the excess water has evaporated.

3. Stir milk and remaining sugar into rice and bean mixture. Cook over medium-low heat, stirring frequently, until very thick, 10 to 15 minutes. Add orange segments and cool, as desired. Before serving, stir in vanilla and sprinkle with cinnamon.

SOYBEAN GRANOLA

This crunchy and chewy treat can be eaten with milk or yogurt for breakfast, or as a snack, anytime. Soybeans are packed with protein and are a delicious and healthful replacement for the nuts of the classic granola.

Preparation time: 10 minutes
Cooking time: 30 to 35 minutes
Makes 3 cups

$^1/_2$ pound cooked soybeans
$1^1/_2$ cups old-fashioned oats
$^1/_2$ cup raisins
$^1/_2$ teaspoon ground cinnamon
Pinch nutmeg
$^1/_4$ cup honey
2 tablespoons molasses
1 tablespoon vegetable oil

1. Preheat oven to 350°F. Place cooked soybeans in a large bowl and cover with plenty of water. Rub beans gently to remove their hulls. Pour off water and hulls. Rinse as necessary. Drain well and dry.

2. Combine beans with oats, raisins, cinnamon, and nutmeg, and set aside.

3. Heat honey, molasses, and oil over a low flame until liquidy. Pour mixture over soybeans and oats. Toss gently until completely coated. Pour mixture onto a nonstick baking sheet and bake, tossing gently every 10 minutes, until golden brown, 30 to 35 minutes. Cool.

ABOUT THE AUTHORS

Tamara Holt

An innovative caterer and professional recipe developer, Tamara Holt has a special flair for making healthful foods elegant and easy. Her training includes apprentice work at the New School Culinary Arts Program and recipe development and testing for several well-known cookbook authors. Tamara Holt is also the author of *Broccoli Power* in this series. She lives and works in New York City.

Marilynn Larkin

Marilynn Larkin is an award-winning medical journalist whose articles have appeared in a wide range of national consumer magazines and medical trade publications. She is a contributing editor for *Nutrition Forum* and a former contributing editor for *Health* magazine. She is also the author of two books to be published in the Dell Medical Library, *What You Can Do About Anemia* and *Relief From Chronic Sinusitis*. Marilynn Larkin lives and works in New York City.

INDEX